My Thoughts Exactly
"The Dirt On Gardening"

By
Tom Yoder

Thalictrum House

My Thoughts Exactly
"The Dirt On Gardening"

Published by Thalictrum House

Dedication

I dedicate this book to my wife Beverly whose love, patience, and inspiration have motivated me and my efforts — and to the reading public who encourage me with kind words and adulation.

TABLE OF CONTENTS

My Thoughts Exactly
"The Dirt On Gardening"

HISTORY

WHAT DOES MOTHER'S DAY MEAN TO YOU?

Hugs, kisses, remembrances, broad smiles, family meals or sometimes eating out, bouquets of flowers, or a beautiful flowering plant, or mushrooms? Actually, they all apply to most of us.

Remembering your mom always conjures up memories of the past as well as the present — it's an inbred thing I guess.

With me, as a child, it was usually a Sunday meal out at a nice restaurant — something we rarely did except when it was a special occasion. I grew up right after the depression and money was tight for everyone but dad made it happen for the family.

My mom was an inspiration to us as well as to most who knew her — hardworking, kind, loving, and always willing to help someone. She always seemed to be the 'go to person' whenever a need would arise.

Things haven't changed, as can be witnessed, in our present everyday life as we see emblazoned on signs 'HI MOM' or simply the same words mouthed with a wave when caught on camera or TV.

Another adventurous yearly event that happened on or around Mother's Day was always a two or three day trip to the northern woods of Michigan for mushroom hunting. We would pack four or five (myself, my parents, and another couple) into the car and head north.

The roads back then were skinny, two lane, and heavily traveled — especially during mushroom season. What now takes us 2 ½ to 3 hours to get to Cadillac, back then took us 4 1/2 to 5 hours because of the curvy, hilly terrain and the slow movement of camper after camper on two lane roads that were heading for the same woods to spend a week of hunting. Deep in the northern forests it was nothing to see ten or fifteen of these early travel trailers or truck campers gathered in a single area much like current campgrounds. Campfires and grills were the norm for cooking breakfast and other meals as well as to snuggle around when temperatures could reach in the 30's and 40's at night.

Dutch Elm disease was rampant in the 40's and 50's and it was not unusual to bring several bushels of black, gray, and yellow morels home to dry or freeze. It's a shame to lose all the Elm to this disease, but it would produce seas of golden morels. Currently, we go north even further to Petoskey where most of the 'finds' are around Black Ash trees — also stressed with disease.

I have pictures of my mother and a friend in her kitchen with dishpans and containers sitting everywhere filled with morels they were cleaning — all fifteen bushels of them from one of the trips north — yes, it's hard to believe but pictures don't lie.

Moms are special and deserve recognition on their calendar day with a hug, a kiss, a bouquet of flowers, a plant, a special meal out, or all of the above.

A trip to the florist, garden center, or store will produce a bevy of suggestions and ideas for that perfect gift that will make "MOM" glow with pride. Better yet, plan a meal out to relieve her in the kitchen as well.

Happy Mother's Day Moms!

GRAPES ARE A PASSION IN SOUTHWEST MICHIGAN

Lake Michigan has an impact on the rolling hills of southwest Michigan for grape growers. All the way from the Indiana/Michigan state line, north to the Kalamazoo river, and west to the city of Kalamazoo, where the bulk of the growing is done, moist lake breezes prevent the extremes of heat and cold in the spring and summer months. That same breeze creates "lake effect" snow in the winter months for heavier snow cover and protection of vital roots.

This environment is well known by producers of grape products. It is this very reason that, long ago, winemakers realized this similarity to some of the finest wine growing areas of Germany and France and brought European stock to the area to be planted. Since then wineries have sprouted up all throughout that area with wine tasting stations in abundance to entice the traveling public and has become a major tourism drumbeat.

Wine, however, isn't the only product produced by grape growers. The majority of the 12,000 plus acres that are planted in that area belong to a Co-op called Welch's that contract with area growers to produce Concord (a blue grape) and Niagara (a white grape) for the production of non-alcoholic grape juice and jelly. I pass this facility almost weekly in the town of Lawton, Michigan and its size is quite impressive. Large vineyards are in abundance along SR 40 in this area. Wine grape acreage in Michigan is currently concentrated in four counties — Berrien, Van Buren, Leelanau, and Grand Traverse.

A little farther to the north in the city of Paw Paw is one of the area's largest and well known wineries — St Julian's. Tours are available on request to give visitors insight into the production procedures. A wine tasting counter gives customers a chance to taste the many different varieties before purchasing. Most are available also at stores locally as well as throughout the U.S.

Lake Michigan is 307 miles long and 118 miles wide and is the sixth largest fresh water lake in the world. The whole eastern lakeshore is ideal for growers because of its near perfect environment for fruits and vegetables and its consistent annual rainfall that produces juicy crops.

This area leads the nation in tart cherry production, especially in the northern parts of the state. A lifetime friend of mine many times would bring me a bottle of cherry wine when returning from there — always a favorite. Other major fruit crops grown along the lake are apples, peaches, pears, and blueberries.

While buying fruit for my employer at these growers, the bulk of the purchases were all the many varieties of apples and peaches. It was nothing to have more than a dozen different varieties of apples and half a dozen varieties of peaches. These same fruits were shipped all throughout the Midwest by the grower with many 'Chicago-land' trucks frequenting these growers for their own venues in the big city. These growers, while depending on their basic crop, didn't rely solely on just fruit — they nearly always grew vegetables or a pumpkin crop just in case of a crop failure because of a late freeze that would render them helpless or less than a normal year.

APRIL SHOWERS BRING MAY FLOWERS

You've no doubt heard that old adage as a child and it still rings true. The cold snows of winter suddenly turn to the warm rains of spring encouraging new growth in plant life of all kinds.

It's important that we keep our flower and vegetable plants watered especially when they are first rooting and establishing deeper footing. Sprinklers do a fine job and are important but there is just nothing better than a good soaking from a warm spring rain. I can't explain it other than it must be the deep soaking of a rain that seems to do a much better job at hydrating plants.

Step outside after a good downpour with the clouds fading away and the sun re-emerging — all the dust in the air has been removed and everything seems brighter, fresher, and pure again.

Conservation is reviving our interest in water retention with the use of rain-barrels for watering our gardens and supplementing our household uses. Local programs have been initiated and to create even more interest they have incorporated a rain-barrel painting contest that includes prizes and an auctioning of the barrels.

This practice was normal in years gone by, especially by farmers. It was not unusual to see old wooden barrels or other makeshift containers that would 'catch' rain run-off from a farmhouse or barn. The ladies loved this softer water to wash their hair in and to do their laundry in as well. Well drilling came next and pumps incorporated to fill cisterns or holding tanks.

My grandfather's farmhouse had a cistern in a back room that was at least six feet wide and quite deep. This room was their "clean-up" area when coming in from the barn or the fields and had a hand pump installed to pump fresh water from the cistern. It was crystal clear, cold, and drinkable and always welcomed after coming in from the hot and dirty fields or the barn after pitching hay for the many cows and horses. Of course back then they even made their own soap out of fat and tallow and lye. As a child I can still remember my mother making soap in this fashion and always had these brown chunks of it lying around in the laundry area — it resembled the old Fels Naptha brand that you could purchase at your grocers.

Water is a resource that should be taken seriously with conservation and steps taken to keep it from being contaminated by bad practices of everyone.

Chemical run-off from lawns and farms that border streams and waterways is always a concern for contamination. A buffer zone that allows water to penetrate the surface would be advised so that any applied chemicals can be filtered through the soil before entering the waterways. Unscrupulous dumping of trash and debris in and around lakes and streams is yet another source of water contamination.

Good responsibility by everyone will help keep our streams and lakes and waterways cleaner for us, our children, and all our wildlife.

A stroll in the woods after a warm spring rain will just about always produce wildflower sightings and mayflowers — it may also, if you're lucky enough, produce an even rarer sighting — morel mushrooms.

SOME THINGS NEVER CHANGE AND THAT CAN BE A GOOD THING

When roaming the countryside of northern Indiana and lower Michigan one might sense they have returned to the past — say the 40's and earlier of yesteryear. All seems to remain the same year after year — especially the farming practices of many that farm the area. Well, basically they haven't on many of these farms.

We would be referring to our good friends and neighbors in the Amish communities that dot the countryside — especially in LaGrange and Elkhart counties. These traditions remain, for the most part, by doing things 'the old fashion way'.

Many of the back roads from Goshen, Indiana to Shipshewana, Indiana remain the same but for some new construction of simple, usually white, frame homes that will house the newly married sons and daughters of Amish farmers or, quite often, these newlyweds will occupy the old farmstead home and the elderly owners will build their retirement home right next door. But, for the most part, these old homesteads have been there for as long as I can remember (and that would be quite a while).

When growing up south of Middlebury, Indiana we lived just across the road from an Amish farm family so I got indoctrinated to the Amish way of life at an early age. Buggy rides and pony carts were nearly an everyday event as my Amish playmates were close to the same ages as me and my siblings. In fact you can go back just three generations on my father's mother's side of the family to be of Amish descent.

My grandfather on the Yoder side was one of the first preachers and originators of the old Warren Street Mennonite Church that sat behind Varn's and Hoover's Hardware in Middlebury. Of course, it is now gone and the land is part of the hardware store property. He was also a school teacher at the, now gone, one room 'Sanitary' School (strange name for a school but so it was) that sat across the road from Middlebury Produce between Middlebury and Shipshewana.

Now talk about prolificacy — this man also farmed a good deal of acreage northwest of Middlebury with a team of horses, and had the usual farm animals found on any farm- milking cows, beef cattle, hogs, and chickens — his large (and mean) bull was kept in a separate fenced area with a big bronze nose ring in his nose. I still have records, handed down from my father, of cattle that was born, bought, or sold by him.

I spent many hours in the barn helping milk the cows on a three legged stool that they would just love to kick out from under me. I was young enough that they scared me to death but the most fun was squirting direct 'hits' at the cats that just loved the warm milk.

In the summer months I would go to the fields and harrow for grandpa with his team of horses (Bess & Jake as I recall) by riding on a flat board atop the harrow. I was too young to do any plowing but was amazed at the commands (gee & haw) I gave to the horses that would be obeyed giving me a sense of power — Ha!

In the fall we all returned to the fields with sickles, cutting rows of corn by hand (back then you could easily walk between the rows). Then came the husking performed with an instrument strapped on your hand with a short metal blade that made it easier to remove the husk from the ear of corn. This was followed with gathering a number of stalks and 'bunching' them together with binder-twine followed with stacking them 'teepee style' into shocks with one placed across the top to help divert rain away from the center.

This reminiscence of shocking corn brings to mind 'fall' each year and the use of corn shocks for decorating. Nothing says 'fall' more than a few stalks of corn with an ear or two dangling and some well-placed pumpkins, gourds, and mums on a bale of straw — maybe even toss in a scarecrow for good measure to add a whimsical touch.

I'M A TRADITIONALIST

Some have their own theories and I have mine (I guess it's called "to each his own"), but to me Christmas is a time for celebration, not only for the birth of Jesus, but also the family and the passed -down traditions of years gone by.

It was expected, for as long as I can remember (80 years and counting), to celebrate this holiday with the traditional Christmas tree, exchanging of gifts, and laughter and excitement. To me it just isn't Christmas without it.

Now, as I age, my wife and I celebrate on Christmas Eve to allow our children, grandchildren, and great-grandchildren their individual Christmases and morning excitement — one might say "the torch has been passed".

While we could still hold these activities at our home, which we used to do, we now rent a hall because of the increasing size of our extended family (thirty-five to forty and growing) and the convenience it offers. Our condo is on two different levels which meant that some were up and some were down and that, quite often, meant kids were on one level and adults on another — the hall makes it perfect.

As a child it was always something us kids looked forward to. My parents would tease us with hints of what 'maybe' was coming and the excitement would increase each day leading up to that eventful "Christmas morning". It never had to be much, just a special toy or a 'had-to-have' that made our day. Sometimes it was a 'sneak-peek' in the closet where gifts were hidden only to be reprimanded that Santa was watching and the gifts were going to go away.

When my wife and I were first married, my wife introduced a new form of teasing with one "shaker gift" that could be shaken once it appeared under the tree. Every day each child (all six of them) could shake their gift and guess what it might be. If the guess was correct they would get to open it as an early gift. This activity was aggravated by concealing or dummying the gift by placing it in a tube or a larger -than-necessary box. It was as exciting as opening gifts on Christmas morning and always gave them something to look forward to each year. They still talk about it — you too should give it a try.

My wife and I have graduated to (or dumbed down to) the artificial tree, mainly because it takes less work to erect and less clean-up after the holidays although I still do miss the scent of a fresh pine tree and the less than perfect form. A store-bought artificial tree is just 'too' perfect.

However, once they're decorated with a gazillion ornaments accumulated over decades and the beaded ropes, ribbons, and the angel topper they will all look pretty much the same.

If you're purchasing a fresh cut tree from a local vendor make sure that it is what they say "fresh cut". Tree life varies with the weather conditions since they were cut but normally they will last five to six weeks without losing needles if 'prepped' correctly before taken indoors.

If your tree hasn't been 'shaken' properly when purchased then bounce it on a hard surface several times to loosen and remove dead needles that have lodged on the inside branches. Saw an inch or more off the bottom of the trunk (this is important) to expose fresh wood and then place the tree in a bucket of water overnight. Try the aspirin trick by putting several aspirin in the water bucket — it is said that it will help absorption and quicken the hydration.

Once inside and mounted in a tree stand make sure that the trunk easily reaches the water reservoir. It's most important to keep a daily vigil on the reservoir so that there will always be water available for the tree — especially the first few days.

Once the holiday is over and needles begin to dry and fall it's best to remove it to the outside to remove the fire hazard.

SAVE A FAVORITE PLANT

Did you have a favorite plant this year or in a past year that you just couldn't get enough of? This often is the case and we literally hate to give it up at season end. It had perfect blooms with magnificent foliage and thrived and expanded better than all the other plants.

We all have our favorites and try each year to expand on the particular beauty of a specimen but sometimes there is that one that you just marvel at.

Sure, you can wait until the following year in hopes to find that same plant or, you can take cuttings and carry them through the winter months so that when spring arrives you'll be prepared to transplant them into your favorite pot or urn or in the garden.

While perennials can survive in freezing weather by mulching them heavily, unfortunately annuals and plants that are out of the warmer planting zones must be removed to the indoors in order for them to survive.

Normally by year's end most of our annuals and perennials have grown much too large to be moved so that leaves us to the next best thing, making cuttings.

Now I'm not at all suggesting you make cuttings of all your annuals and perennials, only a "special" plant or two that you hate to give up — it's relatively easy to do and offers you a wintertime project to keep your thumb green.

Some initial precautions will gain you the best results. A sterile razor works best to take an angled cut three to four inches from the tips of tendrils. Remove the bottom leaves by pinching or snapping them off leaving three or four leaves. Plunge the stem into a planting medium that consists of finely ground peat, perlite, and sand or purchase a product meant for this purpose, then water generously and cover with clear plastic — create a tent by placing sticks in the medium to keep it off the growing plants. Make certain there is adequate drainage in the container.

Once rooting takes place (normally 15-20 days depending on what you're rooting), remove the plastic covering to expose rooted plants to a normal atmosphere.

When the plants develop a sizeable root structure remove them to individual pots of a size that enables them to get somewhat root-bound. Believe it or not a plant will do better with a concentrated root structure — if planted in too large a pot, roots just get stringy and plants suffer.

Taking cuttings aren't restricted to just flowering plants or vines; this may also be done with any "woody" shrub or ornamental, keeping in mind 'time involved' to accomplish a project of this type. This may best be left to nurserymen because it sometimes takes several years to develop any sizeable plant and may even require grafting which is yet another subject.

Experimentation is in a gardener's makeup, I guess that is why new "stuff" is coming on the market every year. The largest growers and developers are constantly hybridizing and searching for yet another prize winner to tantalize us with.

A grower in my hometown (Middlebury, Indiana) by the name of Walter Welch, who lived on a small farm at the western edge of "Witmer Hill" (Wayne Street), grew and very successfully hybridized Irises. He developed the first dwarf Iris in 1950 and created many new colors and strains. He was well known in the horticultural society winning the coveted American Iris Societies Caparne Award with his entry "Primus" (1950), followed by 7 more for the same award — 'April Morn' (1954), 'Blazon' (1955), 'Sparkling Eyes' (1956), 'Veri Gay' (1958), 'Cherry Spot) 1960), 'Fashion Lady' (1964), and 'Atomic Blue' (1965). I was always amazed at his dedication and work ethic.

A WALK DOWN MEMORY LANE

Having lived only a block from these famous gardens, I made a visit recently that took me back 70 years when I used to walk barefoot through this World's Fair re-incarnated nursery exhibit.

Vernon Krider, founder of Krider Nurseries in Middlebury, brought his exhibit back home from the 1933/1934 Chicago World's Fair and had the forethought to re-construct it in 1935 directly across the road from his nursery business. At that time they were one of the largest employers in town and the reason Middlebury was able to secure one of the largest Post Offices of that time because of the volume of nursery stock that was shipped through the Postal Service.

Reconstructing the exhibit was not a simple task but one that took many, many days because of its grandiose and formal design. He wanted it to be a focal point for everyone visiting his nursery business and one that would give each person that wandered through it a sense of peace and amazement.

What made it so exciting back then were the unusual features throughout the stroll thru the gardens. Every turn drew a new and unbelievable chill down the spine with little nooks of overhanging flowers or a secluded bench to rest.

As I recall, back then there were two large ponds, each had beautiful lilies with lily pads covering a good portion of the surface, but not enough to inhibit the excitement of watching the goldfish dashing about. Other pond plants enhanced the surface and perimeter with fountains spraying a constant and mesmerizing bounce off the water's surface.

Inching one's way along the formal design would bring sigh after sigh of the beauty. This was a showcase of everything the nursery had to offer and why it was so successful.

There was a large rose garden with all the favorites as well as newer introductions of hybrid teas (the thornless red rose was their exclusive patent), perennials throughout including the latest developed varieties available, and an abundance of annuals to enhance every turn.

Mid-way through the exhibit was one of the most unusual displays anyone had ever seen — a giant toadstool tall enough to gather under with several smaller ones that one could sit on. It became a photographer's magnet — everyone with a camera had to shutter their family or friends under the giant toadstool — oh what fun!

The anchor 'extraordinaire' at the very rear of the exhibit was an amazing replication of a Dutch windmill. How exciting! This, along with the giant toadstool display was reproduced on catalogs and brochures sent to many, many inquiring clients.

This became a summer job to many youngsters in Middlebury who would "stuff" catalogs and brochures to be sent to inquiries throughout the United States and abroad. I took my turn at this as well.

While the formal design of the gardens is gone and a memory, it has been re-incarnated as a glorious park. With the help of the Middlebury Parks Dept. and many volunteers it has become a focal point yet again that will take your breath away with its wondering pathways that include perennials galore, spring flowering bulbs, blossoming trees of all kinds, a quilt garden, and at this writing much of it in bloom.

Last year I presented an 8 X 11 picture to the president of the volunteer group that I had taken circa 1960 at the entrance to the formal gardens — it may be in the historical museum across the road from the park.

If you're looking for a serene afternoon someday, take a stroll thru this park — and be sure to take your camera.

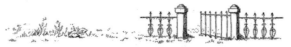

TRAVEL

ARE TROPICAL PLANTS YOUR NICHE

While not an expert in this class of plants, I've always admired them. There seems to be many more unusual species found in tropical plants than the normal outdoor Indiana plant life. Maybe I just feel this way because it's not what I normally was used to seeing in the day to day activity at the garden center.

Tropical gardening in our area, or for that matter anywhere other than the tropics, takes special handling and a good deal more knowledge than the average gardener has. The delicacy of the plants and blooms are what makes them a little more special to a flower lover.

An Elkhart, Indiana native, taking the Master Gardener Course the same time that I did, was 'this' expert at growing tropical plants. This was her niche and she grew many varieties of Orchids that she would proudly 'show-off' at garden shows or the yearly garden walks.

Tropical plants characteristics are just a little different than our garden variety plants in that they are strikingly unusual in shape, growing habits, and just plain beauty. Not many can say that they aren't impressed when seeing a delicate orchid of multiple soft colors and fragrance that are fit for a King. One might think the Orchid would be the state flower of Hawaii instead of the tropical yellow Hibiscus — after all, aren't the infamous 'leis' of that state made of Orchids?

When first stepping off the plane in Hawaii years ago the first order of business was to be adorned with beautiful Orchid leis on each passenger. In fact, as I recall, every stewardess wore an orchid lei on the flight to Hawaii along with the traditional 'flower motif' garment.

The first step off the plane was truly unbelievable coming from zero conditions of the Midwest in December to, "as they say", a tropical paradise of balmy breezes and 80 plus degrees made it easily understandable why tropical plants flourish in this atmosphere.

At our hotel dining room, pink and purple Orchids lying on ice adorned every square inch of the forty foot long buffet table that wasn't occupied with a tempting dish only to be dismantled after each meal and lovingly replaced with fresh orchids for the next meal — indeed fit of a king's ransom.

Of course Orchids aren't the only flowers growing in this tropical paradise — there are many other equally beautiful flowers as well as green plants, some of them giant behemoths that grow wild in the mountains.

While on a hike in the mountains through one of their many parks an amazing thing happened — what started as a fine mist progressively turned into a torrential downpour that made us run for shelter. Other than a good soaking, the experience of the warm rain was taken all in laughter and the experience of the moment. As on all of the islands, the rains are short lived and the re-emerging sun quickly dries you off.

Locally, other than a few personal privately owned greenhouses, one would have to seek out a botanical garden to see these rare gems. There are a few that may be found that aren't too distant — the Ft. Wayne, Indiana Botanical Gardens and the Wellfield Botanical Gardens in Elkhart, Indiana or drive a little farther to Grand Rapids, Michigan to the Meijer Gardens and the Tropical Conservatory — this five story structure features tropical plants from five continents of the world as well as waterfalls and misty steam beds.

VACATIONS BRING LUSTER OF A FLOWERING KIND

The winter doldrums are an inherent aspect of the day to day drudgery and the snow, the slush, and the freezing grip of the season.

As a kid, however, it was just another day and I would relish the thought of climbing that hill to sled or toboggan or ski and to get right back up and do it again and again. In more recent years it's tubing which looks like fun but I never had the chance to enjoy that new sport.

Everyone had their perfect spot for their winter activities and sometimes several of them. My favorite spot was the "Krider hill" in Middlebury that loomed directly behind the infamous Krider's Nursery offices and warehouse. Another plus was that it was only a block from where I grew up.

There aren't too many hills of this height, slope, and length around anymore as most (including this one) are now developed and privately owned. Now we rely on a city park such as the Abshire Park or commercial facilities such as Swiss Valley Ski Lodge in Jones, Michigan. to satisfy our urge for winter fun.

With the fears of a liability suit, and the increased insurance costs to protect owners, many of the old standbys are a thing of the past.

Well, what's the next best thing to enjoying winter sports — how about a winter vacation?

A trip to Florida where temps are more acceptable and short sleeves and shorts abound are a welcome respite from snow boots and hoodies of our north. It doesn't have to be a lengthy stay (although the more the merrier) but enough to thaw out and remember what is to come in another couple of months back here in Indiana.

It also lets us get up close to the southern Mother Nature's greenery and colorful blossoms again. It would always put a smile on my face to see blossoming again while visiting the south when we were knee deep in snow in the north.

Winter vacation points of interest that offer relief from our cold might include the islands of the Caribbean or many of the southern or southwestern states — of course California (much like Florida) is always balmy (or is it)? Judging from reports at this writing they are all colder than we are. Now that's scary!

Wintering in the warmer climates of some of our southern and western states is a common practice for many, as it was for my wife and me for a number of years in Arizona, and it was always a treasure to witness the early blossoming of plants and the green-leafed trees. The commonality of many of the flowers was always a welcome sight but even more intriguing were the many nuances of the southwest plants.

Cactus of all kinds abound at the local nurseries and flea market outlets as well as the rest of the 'staples' in vegetation of the area like the Mesquite Tree and the Cholla (jumping) cactus.

The infamous Saguaro cactus of the Arizona and southern California area, I learned, are a protected species. These I've been told, and some of which are behemoths, cannot be moved under state law without permission from the state and, even then, properly tagged and registered. New highway construction many times made it necessary to move many but they too had to go through the same procedures — normally only moved to the median or outside roadway rights. Some of these giants can weigh in excess of two tons — needless to say requiring heavy equipment to move and care not to damage.

Spring comes early in the southern states and, in the southwest if there is an ample spring rainfall, the mountains are ablaze with wildflowers — a spectacle to behold.

THE HILLS ARE ALIVE

Well maybe not yet, but if you've ever been to the Southwest in the spring, especially after an unusual amount of early year rainfall, the mountains and desert come alive with unbelievable color. It's hard to believe that anything so dry in the summer months could produce wildflowers in such abundance and every color of the rainbow and so unusual that they take your breath away.

If you're not up to hiking the hills, there are numerous botanical gardens that you can visit and they have all the flowers tagged with descriptions of each variety.

To capture the real beauty of the Southwest in the spring however, one needs to take a drive, preferably off-roading or the back roads, and get back deep into the hills where nature is basically untouched. That's where you'll capture the best pictures of hillsides draped in color and cactus and wildflowers seething with blooms and color that defy description. Blooming starts early compared with our Midwest flowers — usually starting in March and continuing through April or until the heat of the desert saps the moisture from the ground and every drop of water is for the survival of the plant. Some cactus, like the Saguaro, has the ability to store enormous amounts of water to survive the desert heat — most weighing 3200 to 4800 pounds when fully hydrated. The Saguaro is unique to the Sonoran Desert and grows in a single column until seventy or eighty years old when it will grow appendages (arms) and form the traditional Saguaro shape that is Arizona's trademark. The Saguaro flower is Arizona's state flower. It was once said that a middle-east Sheik so loved the Saguaro that he shipped hundreds to his homeland to be planted in the desert only to have them die before realizing they can only survive in the Sonora Desert.

Prickly Pear cactus, or more commonly known as Paddle Cactus because of their resemblance to the paddle and ball toy, is common throughout the west and produce all colors of blooms from white to lilac to red to purple and to yellow. Even the plant itself changes color from greens to purples to reds. They can be quite attractive when incorporated into a domestic landscape.

Prickly Pear Cactus jelly can be made from the fruit of the plant. Wait until fall when the fruit is red and purple and remove the fruit with metal tongs. Follow on-line recipes to complete the process.

Wild Poppies are probably the most admired flowers in the foothills and desert as they are in such abundance. When seen from a distance, they are awe inspiring. Their colors range from white to yellow to red to orange and create an enormous blanket of color patterns when mixed with other wildflowers. Their pictures are popular on the internet and are even more breathtaking in person.

The Cholla (pronounced choy-yuh) cactus, or sometimes referred to as teddy bear cactus or jumping cactus, is also prominent in the Southwest and is said to be able to "throw" its needles when passing close. The needles are easy to cling with a mere touch of the plant, thereby its reputation for throwing needles. They have a reverse barb making the needles extremely difficult to remove. They produce a flower too but it is rather insignificant bearing colors from green to grey. The plant itself is quite handsome bearing a resemblance to a teddy bear with its fuzzy appendages.

There are many varieties in the cactus family and each is unique in shape and size and each produce their own flower and color. It's the delicate shapes and colors of the flowers that make them even more unusual.

If you ever get the chance, visit the Southwest in the spring and drink in its beauty, you won't be disappointed- especially if the pre-season was a wet one.

GOD'S WORK AND BEAUTY NEVER DISAPPOINT

Every true gardener marvels at nature and what has been created for all of us to enjoy.

It may be our backyard garden of vegetables that miraculously perform year after year with delicious and colorful food for our tables or the fruit trees that burst with colorful spring blooms that are pollinated and swell into luscious fruits of all kinds.

It may be a flower garden that we have meticulously planned and planted then waited for the rains and the sunshine to watch each plant develop into their unique and fragile blossoms.

Look closely at a blossom and marvel at its intricacy — some almost beyond belief. Then watch the bee or the hummingbird or the butterfly taste its nectar and dance from one to the other pollinating as they go.

Marvel at the majestic trees that not only provide us with beautiful vegetation but also comfort in the form of shade and shelter, then in the fall present us with a second performance with some of the most awesome colors on this earth of golden yellows, crimson reds, burnt oranges, and all tinged with what remains of the greens of summer.

If you are a traveler to the south or west it is most interesting to watch the changes in vegetation from state to state. Different temperature zones along your route produce vastly different species, all uniquely beautiful in their own environment.

In the southern states Rhododendrons grow wild and moss hangs gracefully from the trees. Travel south even further and stately palms line the streets and beaches.

Travel west and southwest and you'll encounter vast desert areas intermingled with mountains. Pines at the uppermost levels turn into sage and tumbleweeds in the foothills.

Travel southwest even further and desert plants emerge as you reach the lower altitude levels. Paddle cacti abound as well as the all too familiar stately Saguaro cactus with its outstretched arms.

Traveling along the rural roads of the southwest you're bound to encounter the Teddy Bear Cholla with its 'so called' jumping needles and Ocotillo and Agave.

If you're there in the spring after a wet February or March you can witness some of the most unusual and awesome flowers that these cacti produce — you may not see them every year but the wait is worth it. Unfortunately the blooms are short lived so a camera is a must. The foothills also produce hillsides of wildflowers that rival non-predominantly oranges and purples.

Travel north from the southwest and you'll pass through the Joshua Tree Forest in northern Arizona. These trees always reminded me of something I would encounter in the middle-east centuries ago — small scraggly (almost deformed) trees with tufts of needles at their appendages.

State after state has their own unique and unusual plant life and all are God's work at its best. Then imagine every corner of the earth in its entirety, all with their individual and beautiful plant-life — all I can say is WOW, God is wonderful!

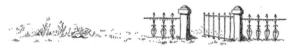

GENERAL GARDENING

I SMILE A LOT

People make me smile by the remarks they make to me when I hit on a subject that is dear to them and it triggers their memory of 'back when' or maybe it is a flower that they too had grown (or still do) and they make a connection.

While I try to help educate the average gardener, I also thrill at the opportunity to get that response of "oh yah, I remember those" or "I used to have one of those". It happens regularly when people see me at the store or on the street and I smile to myself, [another reader of my columns].

My intent is to spark interest in the new gardener and help them in their quest for gardening knowledge and at the same time trigger the seasoned gardener's brain and renew that forgotten thing from their past — you know what they are — "my mom used to grow those" or "we used to have those when I was a kid" kind of answer.

I have to chuckle because I too relate to those past gone days of my "growing up on the old homestead". Of Hollyhocks and Rhubarb patches and corn rows (and they were 24" rows back then) and squash and pumpkin and muskmelon vines everywhere in the garden.

There's something to be said about the old 'standards' (and they still have their place) but new is even more exciting because of hybridizing that creates new and more disease resistant strains of nearly everything. That's why we lead the world in grain production.

New hybrid strains of corn with the best in fertilizers and disease and weed prevention products keeps us at the top and offers us the opportunity to help other nations benefit by teaching them what we already have accomplished. For them to be able to be more self-sufficient is the goal of our endeavors and by doing this it also creates self-satisfaction on their part.

Crops aren't the only things that we benefit from when it comes to 'hybridizing'. New strains of the old standard bearers are introduced every year that are more disease resistant and tweaked for compaction or height to make them more appealing for garden applications to the average gardener.

New colors of flowers are yet another example of hybridizing. Multiple colors on a single blossom can be achieved as well as increased sizes or clustering blossoms — a flat blossom versus a blossom with multiple waves.

These accomplishments aren't only for the satisfaction of the person doing the hybridizing but also to appeal to gardeners the world over.

Man is always on the search for newer and better in all walks of life and agriculture and gardening is one of the most prolific research areas.

My greatest interest is flowers so I'm always interested in what is 'new on the market' in plant releases.

One of the largest hybridizers in the flower industry is "Proven Winners" of California so I'm constantly on the watch for what they have to offer as 'new'. That's why you see so many "PW" tags at all the garden centers each year. They are at the top of the list each year for hybridizing awards — not for only one but for many awards — just Google "Proven Winners" in your search engine on the computer and you'll easily see what I mean — it will make you smile too!

WILL SPRING BE EARLY — MAYBE YES, MAYBE NO

According to Punxsutawney Phil we're going to have an early spring and that makes me somewhat happy. One surely wouldn't know it from the likes of the freezing temperatures outside at this moment.

Having just returned this February from Phoenix, Arizona., where temperatures were in the 70's when leaving, left me somewhat in shock while retrieving my snow and ice laden vehicle in 14 degree temps in a light jacket at the airport then driving home on the US 20 by-pass in extremely nasty weather. (Why did I leave Arizona?).

It has been a roller-coaster ride so far this winter with highs in the fifties and lows in the single digits with thirty degree swings in a twenty-four hour period. The much too early spring could happen again like it did last year although I hope not — an early spring may put a smile on your face but it can render disaster to fruit and vegetable farmers.

These topsy-turvy weather patterns cause significant damage to our local fruit and vegetable industry with total destruction of fruit crops in some cases as it did last year.

Weather patterns very widely in a one hundred mile radius so growers are always on the watch for freezes. Some precautionary measures are available but it's always worrisome that it will not be enough. These fruit growers, understanding the delicate balance of temperatures from bud to maturity in different growing areas, will sometimes 'help' growers that have been hurt by unusual weather circumstances by offering tons of their own crops to tide the grower over for the season. I've seen it happen several times over a fifteen year period where the large peach farmer I frequented had to rely on this 'help' from a grower farther north whose crops were not affected. Thank goodness for this co-operation between growers.

A fruit grower's life is not an easy one. Pesticides must be applied early at what is known as "silver tip" (first emergence of the leaf) and at timed intervals thereafter in order to have disease–free crops, then ripening fruit tested every few days for correct sugar content and ripeness. It's all a matter of timing and weather conditions play an important part. Basically, growers are at the mercy of weather each year during the growing and ripening process.

Nearly all fruit growers who deal in the standard crops of peaches, apples, grapes, cherries, blueberries, apricots, plums, and raspberries hesitate to 'put all their chips in one basket', so to speak, and therefore raise other crops as well like pumpkins, bell peppers, Indian corn, and 'yes' even wheat, soybeans, and hybrid corn crops, which aren't as apt to be affected by wide temperature swings. This practice will soften the blow in case of failure in one or more of their prime fruit crops.

Seed catalogs are in the mail and entertaining orders — massive seed displays will soon (if not already) be on the floors of every entity that deals in gardening. Greenhouse operations are gearing up for March deliveries of planting material which will kick-off the growing season for this year. Sound unbelievable?- well it's true — only a month away when greenhouses will start bursting with newly planted green life.

To me, and to the majority of gardeners, there is no sweeter smell than to step into a greenhouse of 68 to 70 degree temperatures in the middle of winter. The moisture-laden air and the smell of planting medium (grower's dirt) will lift the spirit and make you forget the winter blues.

Don't despair — 30 days isn't that far away and we all know April (60 days) is planting time for early flowers and vegetables like pansies and violas and cabbage and broccoli.

SPRING HAS SPRUNG

Officially spring arrived on the 20th of March in 2013 and with Easter arriving early this year and Palm Sunday a week prior to that one would think it's time to plant flowers and gardens.

Well, don't get too excited just yet because Mother Nature might have something to say about that.

While yearly calendar events normally dictate when it's time to do certain things such as 4th of July, Memorial Day, Thanksgiving, and Christmas — it's not so when starting or planting vegetables and flowers outside in your garden. There are some events, like Easter, that is dictated by the March equinox and not by the Gregorian calendar or the Julian calendar and so the date is variable, hence planting times can't be relied on solely because it's Easter or Palm Sunday.

A better indicator for planting would be to watch the calendar for the appropriate dates and the weatherman for seasonal fluctuations and more appropriately the ground temperature.

'Good Friday', the Friday preceding Palm Sunday, typically is (according to folklore) the earliest and maybe the perfect time to plant your potatoes. Again, this is best determined by ground temperatures and the soil's tilling readiness — and the 'certified seed potatoes' availability at garden centers.

If frost is still present in the soil (not just the surface but to a depth of several inches) then more than likely tilling is not an option. Give your soil the squeeze test — grab a fistful of dirt and if it retains the mud-ball consistency then it's not yet ready — if it crumbles naturally then it's more than likely ready to till.

With the advent of Easter arriving at this early stage it becomes even more critical to protect newly purchased Easter Lilies from the cold temperatures outside while transporting them from store to home or to the church.

Most stores can supply you with an oversized plastic bag or a large piece of plastic for this purpose — if you're real lucky they may have the grower's protective sleeve that still remains on the plant. Stores that have purchased lily plants from large growers and suppliers will many times simply strip the protective sleeve to the base and leave it there until sold making it easy to pull back up and over the blooms for protection.

Lilies are sensitive to major temperature swings much like another seasonal plant, the Christmas Poinsettia, and require precaution when transporting even for short distances.

Once in the home they prefer, and will do best in, a bright area near a window but not in direct sunlight. Refrain also from placing them near drafts, fireplaces, or heat sources that will diminish their life considerably.

If so desired, these plants may be planted outdoors in a garden once temperatures will allow. As in indoors, they prefer a lot of light but not direct sunlight with cool feet. This can be accomplished with a heavy mulching or with a groundcover or a bed of crocus. Plan on incorporating a fertile planting soil in the prepared hole and plant mounded so that drainage is established. Once planted, fertilize with a slow release fertilizer monthly, continue to water regularly, and allow foliage to die back naturally to replenish the bulbs. These lilies will establish themselves well and may be enjoyed for many years.

IF YOU'RE NEW TO GARDENING DON'T DISMAY

There is a gardener in everyone just waiting to explore. It only takes one successful episode to transform a "want to be" into a venturesome and inspired grower. Success breeds confidence in any venture and gardening is no different so don't hold back — get your hands dirty this year and plant something — or plant a lot.

Community gardens are ripe for volunteers and much can be learned by working side by side with some of the more seasoned veterans. You'll not only be learning but you'll be serving the community by putting food on someone's table, including your own if you don't have space for your own garden. If you're planning your own garden, plant a little extra to share with your family, friends, church community, and the less fortunate — the rewards are permanent.

The snow may be flying and thoughts of spring may be far away but believe it or not seeds are arriving at stores throughout the area. Generally speaking February brings seed racks to the floors of all the big box stores to pique the interest of the snoring gardeners and build enthusiasm for the up and coming season. Thousands and thousands of seed packets will be sold and it is my belief this year will produce a landmark sales record because of rising vegetable prices.

Many will elect to purchase plants from their local greenhouses rather than start seeds early, but whatever the case may be, plan early to get your "choice" of plants. If you have special wants as far as a specific variety, then you might want to examine all the seed racks thoroughly or order your seeds from a seed catalog. Obviously local greenhouses can't stock every variety.

Start seeds in a soilless potting medium such as Miracle Grow Potting Mix (a mixture of ground bark and peat). When seedlings reach an inch to an inch and a half, transplant into a liner with 1 to 1 ½ inch squares. These small spaces will encourage a tight root development. When plants reach three to four inches with four to five leaves and root development is sufficient, remove to a slightly larger pot. You may want to pinch plants back to encourage branching but always leave at least two leaves. All this should be done with strict sanitation to discourage disease. This is especially true if handling food — always wash hands thoroughly before returning to work with your plants.

Time the planting to start approximately six to eight weeks before the last frost date. Timing can vary in our area by several weeks but a good rule of thumb is not to plant in the garden before mid-May except for cold-hardy plants such as cabbage, lettuce, broccoli and the like.

Want to try something a little different this year? I grew at the green-house for several years a tomato by Burpee called "Tumbler Hybrid" that was grown in a hanging basket. It was a prolific producer of 1" to 1 1/4 "tomatoes with plants that were bushel basket size. The number of tomatoes on a single plant would reach two to three dozen by spraying blossoms with a liquid pollinator. You'll no doubt have to special order from the Burpee Catalog. My only conundrum was they grew so large that I lacked space when fully grown and all this in a few weeks with ripe fruit in less than fifty days.

Another gem is Burpee's "Fourth of July" hybrid that matures equally as fast (49 days) with fruit clusters similar to the "Sweet 100" but a larger 6 oz. fruit size.

Be the early bird and get "first choice" at your seed retailer.

WHAT MAKES A NEW YEAR SPECIAL

Each year brings new anticipation for the season to come. At this time of year one can only dream of the rebirth of the coming season when once again, as in past years, dreams of green grass, budding trees, and spring blooms gives us a spiritual lift and replenishes our undying faith in mother nature.

While we're waiting for the green of spring, why not enjoy the winter beauty that Mother Nature provides us like the snowy tips on an evergreen tree or a rushing stream with overhanging boughs laden with snow or a giggling child's snowman that was erected with the help of a parent.

There are so many things to be thankful for — we're still here and enjoying life, right? (Even though the Mayan calendar told us it would be the end of the world on 12/21/12- the apocalypse theory!).

If we are dealt snow we'll play in it, or (grumble) shovel it or push vehicles in it. Depending on your agility you will ski on it or sled on it or snowmobile on it. The frozen variety will lend you the ability to skate on it (or fall on it — 'that agility thing again').

While most of these activities are man-made and recreational to wile our time away until spring (albeit they are extremely fun), in all actuality it is Mother Nature's way of replenishing the soil with moisture for the coming growing season.

Moisture is an essential for any living thing — without it there would be no vegetation and no 'us'. Without moisture there would be no rivers or oceans or streams or wildlife — in fact you might say moisture is the single most important part of nature.

The point I'm making is, grumble all you want about shoveling and chipping and sloshing and shivering, nature is just trying to replenish the earth with life-giving moisture that will replenish vegetation and grow our crops and make our gardens grow with fresh vegetables and fruit, even though it is in the form of white cold fluff or frozen ice.

Too bad moisture can't be evenly distributed all over the earth (at one point in time billions of years ago it very well may have been) but this is why most towns and cities are located near rivers and streams or adjacent to a large body of water because of the easy access to water — every living thing requires it.

When cities grow beyond their ability to supply the masses with their water requirements, then it becomes necessary to pipe in more, construct reservoirs, or build canals to get it there. Large cities in the desert southwest, like Phoenix and Tucson, have outgrown their ability to supply the masses with water requirements and pay dearly to have it supplied via canals even though they have massive reservoirs. Recent draughts have diminished reservoir levels in many of the western regions.

This is a classic case of man's desire to dwell (at least in the winter months) in the warmer climates of the south and southwest and populations exploded beyond their abilities to provide the necessary water requirements.

Snow can be one of the most visual delights of nature as it falls from the sky and covers the countryside with a clean fresh blanket of white. On the other hand it has the ability to get under our skin when it comes time to shovel a drive or dig a vehicle out. As a child I couldn't get enough of it because it meant sledding, tobogganing, and snowmen and igloos but as an adult the responsibility fell on me to remove it from drives and sidewalks and it became a chore.

Some adults never outlive the fun and eagerly await the snow and cold season to ski, snowmobile, tube, and toboggan and yes, even ice fish.

ALL GOOD THINGS MUST COME TO AN END

Have you ever heard that expression before?

When it comes to gardening, it all too often is an expression referring to the end of the growing season. Recent cold evening temperatures in the upper 20's and lower 30's is the death knell for most vegetation.

There will be a few survivors of the 'cold weather' variety but fragile succulents like Impatiens and Coleus will be, as they say, "toast".

Warm weather isn't completely gone for the season however — there will be plenty of time to enjoy what's left of our spring and summer efforts.

Now would be a great time to start the clean-up process in our gardens by removing dead or browning foliage in preparation for the final winter blanket in a few weeks. This will involve a heavy mulching of leaves (which may be left whole or finely ground) or bark, or peat, or a combination of all along with some well-rotted compost. This 'tea' will bolster your soil's composition and rejuvenate it for the coming year. Next spring, before tilling, add more well-rotted compost. It will not only give you much needed additional nitrogen but will also help to 'lighten' your soil by loosening the compaction and giving you a great 'loamy' mix.

Valuable patio flower containers should be monitored closely and removed to a closed area when temperatures dip below freezing to prevent cracking when the soil expands. I hesitate destroying my pretty flowers in containers this early in the fall season so I'll just keep a close watch and take them in when necessary.

Tea roses are so pretty this time of year but in another week or two it will be time to cut them down to a foot or so and mulch them heavily with leaves and soil covering them completely. Next spring, after all danger of a late freeze, you may cut them back even further after removing the soil and mulch. Trim back, to six inches or so, to green healthy canes remembering always to cut just above an outside bud to retain a candelabra shape. Remove any dead wood down to healthy stock. If you wish, cones may be purchased to 'winterize' your valuable tea roses. Grandiflora and floribunda roses weather the cold temperatures somewhat better and may be shaped and pruned now or in the spring in moderation. Never 'butch' a shrub of this type as they are meant to be grown as a shrub- unlike their counter-part, tea roses. The more recent and highly popular 'knock-out' rose bushes are of this genre' — trim out dead wood and shape moderately.

Another beauty that is still performing well is the fabulous butterfly bush but it too will succumb shortly and then it will be time to cut it back to 1 or 1-1/2 ft. It is very important to mulch this specimen heavily because our, sometimes, sub-zero temps will be too much for them to survive- I've sold some the second time because of negligence in mulching — we're on the edge of its intended zoning limitations. Kept healthy year after year they will grow larger and larger reaching five feet and more becoming a joy to behold and attracting gorgeous butterflies of all colors. I'm especially fond of the deep purple on a mature bush that displays draping fronds measur-ing a foot and a half in length.

Remove your valuable roots, bulbs, and rhizomes from the garden or your patio pots and cull them of rotting or diseased areas, then wash them to remove the soil and thoroughly dry them before storing in dry peat and placing them in a cool and dark spot for winter storage — never store them with apples as it will encourage rot — the ethylene gas emitted from them is the culprit.

In other words, get your house in order because the snow will be flying soon (already is in the upper-peninsula) and it's much more comfortable to be doing these chores now rather than with an inch or two of snow on the ground.

TIME TO CALL IT A WRAP

for the growing season at least. While there may be spurts of warm weather remaining this year, for the most part our season of pretty flowers and luscious vegetables are done because of recent heavy frosts and freezes. If you've been waiting to do those year-end chores of removing frost-damaged annuals or cutting back perennials, roses, butterfly bushes and the like, then now is a good time to start. Evening temperatures in the low and mid-thirties takes its toll on these plants and prepares them for winter hibernation. Trimming them back will help the process by relieving them (so to speak) of supporting the abundant growth while struggling with freezing temperatures.

Mulch your valuable plants with a heavy dose of leaves (or ground up leaves), peat, or bark to protect them from harsh winter winds and freezes. Secure if necessary with a layer of soil, netting, or provide a wind-shield to prevent brisk winds from blowing them bare.

Tea roses may be cut back to ten or twelve inches and dead or unhealthy canes trimmed out, then mulched or provided with "rose cones". Next spring when budding appears, trim back even further, to maybe six or eight inches, to sturdy green canes. Try to retain a candelabra shape by cutting just above healthy outside buds.

Grandiflora and floribunda roses are treated differently. These types of roses are of the cluster variety and grown as a bush. While this type of rose will benefit from a regular yearly pruning, they shouldn't be pruned as severely as a hybrid tea rose. Trim back half to two-thirds of their natural mature size by removing weak branches, old growth, and crossing inner branches. This will encourage new growth while creating air-flow thru the structure. Try to retain the natural rounded shape of this type of bush.

Knock-out roses are of this variety and while there are different recommendations on when best to prune, depending on who you talk to, I'd say either fall or spring — it doesn't really matter. More important is to remove old wood (they bloom on new wood) and thin and shape. Removing spent blooms (an inch or two back) during the growing season will discourage formation of the rounded hops that develop and take away from the beauty. This step also encourages new blossoming.

If you have a Butterfly Bush, cut it back to about a foot and mulch it heavily. They struggle with our sub-zero freezes and need the extra blanket of mulch. If you don't mulch, you will stand the chance of losing it. Next spring when budding begins, you may cut it back further if necessary.

Remove vegetable garden remnants and debris to the compost pile and scatter a fresh supply of well-rotted compost on the garden to be tilled in. Replenish next spring with additional compost to boost the soil's fertility composition and help reduce compaction.

Store your valuable roots, bulbs, and rhizomes by digging, washing, culling, and then drying. Place them in dry peat in a constantly cool (but not freezing) environment like a cool cellar or underground holding area. I place mine in a bag of peat stored in my garage- they've never froze yet and that's with sub-zero temps outside.

In other words, get your house in order, because the snow will be flying soon and I know you don't want to be doing these chores in the snow.

STRAWBERRY FIELDS FOREVER

This is a song by the Beatles written by John Lennon and inspired by Lennon's memories of playing in the garden of a Salvation Army house named Strawberry Field near his childhood home in Woolton — a suburb of Liverpool, England. There has since been a Strawberry Fields memorial constructed in New York City's Central Park named after the song.

The only connection this has to my subject 'strawberries' is that whenever I think about the strawberry fields in our area it conjures up memories of that song that became famous many years ago — I start humming the tune.

Nearly all of us love strawberries — the only fruit, as far as I know, that has their seeds on the outside rather than on the inside of their flesh.

Strawberries are one of the most versatile in the fruit family in that they have so many applications available. Their inclusions are in every dessert book with many recipes that offer up all kinds of delicious dishes whether from fresh, frozen, canned, or dried berries.

Any good restaurant will offer fresh strawberry pie when in season — it may be a double crust with a latticed top, a creamy variety, or a simple whipped cream topping — it may even be a double play that includes rhubarb which is one of my favorites.

Another seasonal favorite that's main ingredient is this delectable fruit is the infamous strawberry shortcake. If you want the genuine variety of shortcake you may have to get help from the 'old school' cooks that made their shortcake the old fashion way — from shortcake that is baked in the oven. It is still the best as far as I'm concerned and it always brings back memories of my mom's.

While pies are always a favorite use, it is only a small fraction of the many, many uses of this versatile fruit. Healthy fruit dishes nearly always have strawberries included — example: fresh peaches, blueberries, raspberries, bananas, seedless grapes, mango, kiwi, and 'strawberries'.

Strawberries dipped in chocolate are a delicacy in most restaurants with some offering a 'chocolate tower' with a liquid waterfall of thick creamy chocolate to dangle your fruit in.

While fresh picked "or purchased" from the field for immediate use is the norm it is certainly not the only reason we pick the fruit. Many families will take their harvest home after picking and prepare them for the freezer to use later and during the winter season. Fresh picked is far and away the best because of their sweeter flavor derived from being 'vine ripened'- unlike their imported sister products that are picked before fully ripened and grown from strains that are more firm and hold up for shipping purposes.

When picking fruit from a "U- pick" grower, the best berries are the ones that have ripened fully but not soft or brown — ones that contain partially white tops are not yet ready to pick. Try to handle the fruit gently and never 'stack' higher than four or five inches — packing higher than this will compress the berries and encourage a shorter life span.

If you are not preparing them immediately upon your return home then refrigeration will be necessary to hold their fresh quality. Normally fresh picked berries will hold up for four or five days refrigerated.

AN APPLE A DAY WILL KEEP THE DOCTOR AWAY — OR SO THEY SAY

This old adage has been around for as long as I can remember and retold generation after generation to children and grandchildren. There's much truth in this old saying and here's why the nutritional value in every apple, as well as the fiber content to help digestion, can help regulate the body's system.

One medium apple contains approximately 110 calories and 150 mg of potassium plus three grams of fiber which is 10 percent of daily intake requirements. While most people think the flesh of the apple is the most delicious part, the skin of the apple is by far the most nutritious. The apple skin contains 4 milligrams of circadian, an anti-oxidant compound preventing oxygen molecules from damaging individual cells. This can prevent cell changes that can lead to cancer and also lowers the risk of heart disease by twenty percent according to a study done in Finland. The study also shows that this compound has been shown to inhibit the growth of tumors and keep cancer cells from spreading. The insoluble fiber in the apple skin is considered roughage and helps the digestive tract run smoothly and helps to prevent diverticulosis, a condition that can lead to colon cancer. Another benefit of insoluble fiber is that it helps as an appetite suppressant by giving you a "full" effect thereby acting as a weight control benefit.

Apples also contain soluble fiber, which has the opposite effect of insoluble fiber, forming a gel-like material in the digestive tract that can help lower cholesterol as well as the risk of stroke and heart disease, according to the study.

Apple juice, though containing some iron and potassium, is not a good substitute for fresh apples because it doesn't contain the beneficial compounds circadian and fiber.

Another of the soluble fibers found in apples is called pectin. Pectin reduces the amount of cholesterol produced in the liver, slows digestion, and the rise of blood sugar making it ideal for diabetes patients. Apples bolster the immune system and helps keep blood sugar levels stable.

There are hundreds of varieties of apples, many of which are still in research at universities, and not yet introduced to the marketplace. Some of these researches can take decades to develop and some never will make it to the marketplace. Such is the case with a recent development by the University of Minnesota that almost left a graft fall by the wayside but for a professor that dug it out of some stock to be discarded and decided it needed to be looked at again. Low and behold this "almost discarded" specimen turned out to be one of the most heralded recent new apples, none other than Honey Crisp. If you've never tasted a Honey Crisp then you have a treat in store because they are, as their name implies, crisp and sweet. They also store better than any other apple I know of lasting (under refrigeration) until March of the following year. The only other apple I know of that comes close in storage longevity is Mutsu. The only other apple with as much new "buzz" and acceptance is Gala.

PEACHES ARE A MAINSTAY IN OUR RURAL CULTURE

While the fresh peach season is slowly dwindling there are still peaches available at most growers because of their ability to stretch the season with large coolers and plenty of moisture that will help retain the moisture content in them. Eventually, though, they will lose that precious moisture and develop a mealy texture which makes them less desirable. Fresh off the vine is best to sink your teeth into and there is no other sensation that takes the place of that peach tang with its juices running down your chin and the desire to get another one to gulp down.

Most growers have a unique process of taking fresh picked peaches that have been collected by pickers, in bags, and carefully rolled into large ten bushel bins. Large flatbed trailers are loaded and hauled to the processing area where they are unloaded with forklifts and placed on a vertical cooling rack that allows cool water to flow through the fruit bins to cool down the warm fruit and prepare them for temporary storage in a cooler at temperatures in the mid-thirties. Time is of the essence to get these fruits processed by washing, grading for size, and culling for irregularities and damaged fruit and boxed for shipping while the fruit is still in prime condition.

Local stores as well as dealers as far away as Chicago and Ohio could buy peaches in bin boxes or crates, to re-sell to the public, from these growers and that's what I did in the August through September months for Everett's Grocery Store. It was a job that was really enjoyable and I learned a lot about the process and the different peaches that were grown as well as the friendships with the different growers that I developed. I still make the trip each year to pick up some of my favorites and to renew old friendships. I take them Olympia chocolates or The Nut Shoppe nuts and candies and they oblige me with peaches or apples — (I love it).

Our local Amish communities are big buyers at these growers with "haulers" that will take orders from their surrounding area and a date set for pick-up and then sell for a modest fee for pick-up and delivery.

Red Haven peaches are still the standard bearer, even with the introduction of many new varieties, because of their unique characteristic of not turning brown after cutting their flesh which makes them ideal for canning and freezing. A pectin can have the same effect on fresh cut peaches by helping to retain the natural color of the fruit's flesh. A fairly new introduction to the market was Paul Friday's "Flaming Fury" — a genetically crossed cultivar that had a lot of the same characteristics as Red Haven by not turning brown when exposed to air. It had a somewhat redder flesh and the taste and quality were superior to some of its rivals.

When Red Haven are no longer available try some of the other or later varieties such as Redskin, Red Star, Coral Star, or Star Fire. If you have never tried a white flesh peach, try one of the newly developed "whites" like Blushing Star — they are wonderful.

Baby Gold peaches, while being a cling variety, are grown sparingly but can still be found and are a favorite for canning because slices retain their shape and color in a canning jar and make an excellent choice for judging in competition. Store bought canned tins are usually of this genre.

Harmony and Loring were eye catchers some years ago with Harmony's beautiful color and size and Loring's huge size and yellow skin. They are mostly gone now though because their size made them easily bruised and less desirable for growers as well as buyers.

HEALTH AND WELLNESS GO HAND IN HAND WITH GARDENING

Ponder this; fresh vegetables, colorful flowers, exercise, and peace of mind will help contribute to your overall health. This is derived, and possibly unknowingly, by the simple act of gardening of all kinds but mostly vegetable gardening.

Nutritionists unrelentingly urge us to eat vegetables, especially the green variety, but also any of the other colorful and healthy vegetables that are grown in most gardens. What better way for us to obtain the substantial values of 'fresh' than those offered from one's own garden?

The exercise one gains from gardening is akin to exercise gained from running, squats, toe-touching, stretches, and many other routines in a regular exercise program. After a day or two of working in the garden or on the lawn, muscles tend to scream because they haven't been used over the winter months — that is unless you regularly exercise at a gym or exercise center. Then in a week or so, after the pain subsides, you feel great and full of energy. This is a phenomenon that athletes and runners find exists when training daily to build muscle and lose fat — this 'need to continue' almost becomes an obsession. Idleness is the devil's advocate so, young or old, exercise or just get out and walk — it will tone your muscles and get all the joints working — of course, always consult your doctor first to make sure you're healthy enough to do this.

Most of us can remember when our mothers would say "eat your vegetables" and we would wince with pain, especially if it was something that we hated. Kids are all alike and have their favorites and dislikes but 'like it or not' mothers do know best and are only trying to do what is best for their children.

Another phenomenon, and most of us will likely relate to this, is the change in our tastes as adults — what we hated most as children turns out to be our favorites as adults. Women who become pregnant and give birth have urges for unusual foods or foods that they never liked before becoming pregnant, but then becomes a favorite after the pregnancy.

I used to sit at the dinner table 'after hours' because I couldn't stomach spinach. As an adult I crave spinach and always want a double helping. There are many other examples of cravings of foods which as a child were ignored or fed (under the table) to the family dog. I'm of the belief that our body's requirements somehow turn the tables on those dislikes and make them acceptable as an adult. Another odd one for me was cooked carrots, which any nutritionist will tell you are one of the healthiest — to me, when a child, they were terrible but I loved them raw and fresh out of the garden — an oddity to be sure.

Now, as adults, we tend to plant our gardens with the things that we crave and change those only when trying a 'new on the market' item. We choose the things that are healthy, tasty, colorful, and easy to prepare. It makes sense to grow our own things to help control family costs and to make them readily available outside our back door.

Gardening takes time, which most of say we have little of, but it is time well spent. Who wouldn't want fresh sweet corn that we grew ourselves or broccoli, cauliflower, zucchini, tomatoes, or cucumbers?

The act of gardening consists of tilling of the soil, preparation of the seed bed, and sowing of the seeds — sounds simple enough and it usually is. The follow up of supports for tomatoes, beans, and other climbers comes shortly after. The real 'rub' and unfortunately the most ignored is weeding and harrowing once things start to grow and expand. Weeds take valuable nutrition and moisture from the plants and, when left to grow, will generally outperform them, not to mention give the garden an unkempt look.

Some of the older generation who still like to garden but find it harder to do the bending that they used to do may find it helpful to raise their beds. Raised beds are becoming more and more popular because of their ease of access. A foot off the ground in a confined area is much more adaptable for anyone, but especially seniors. Make them narrow enough to gain easy access from either side without stepping foot in them.

Take it another step and go skyward with wire cylindrical towers made out of fencing for vining plants like beans and cucumbers. Use steel Shepard hooks to hang a basket cherry tomato plant. Tepee structures made out of simple tree branch sticks are innovative as well as useful for climbing beans or peas.

While exercise is the predominant theme in gardening along with the eventual harvest, its attributes exist in the health and wellness of our bodies.

Our Greencroft Retirement Community is a prime example of this. The management has seen fit to provide residents with garden space that not only offer self-satisfaction but also the much needed exercise that these seniors require. If you think pride isn't important to these gardeners, just take a stroll through their gardens — they are all near perfection and at some of their ages it is quite an accomplishment.

If you haven't tried this, it's time you do for a simple and healthy summer dish:

2 zucchini, young tender two inch diameter

Virgin olive oil

Garlic salt and onion salt

Discard ends of zucchini and slice lengthwise in 3/8th inch slices — don't peel

Dip in or brush on olive oil

Place on a grill (medium heat) and sprinkle with garlic salt, onion salt, and Mrs. Grass's garlic herb seasoning

Turn once after two or three minutes and continue cooking for another two or three minutes — don't overcook, should be only somewhat limp.

Enjoy!

PLANTS PRODUCE MORE THAN COLORFUL FLOWERS

While colorful flowers are the primary reason that we search for plants each spring, some gardeners go the next step and plant for scent of the foliage. Each plant and species has their own unique scent — some much more than others.

Searching for scent becomes an art in itself because of the individuality of each plant. In fact, some plants have no significant blossom but are grown only for the scent of the foliage.

Marigolds, while beautiful in their own right, have a distinct pungent odor which many say (experts included) is a deterrent to many insects and animal life, acting as a biological barrier for gardens, especially vegetable gardens.

Most, however, are grown for the pleasant scent they emit of their own accord or by gently rubbing the foliage.

There are numerous cultivars that produce lemon fragrances like lemon mint, lemon thyme, lemon scented Verbena, and lemon scented Geraniums — in fact, an extremely popular scented Geranium is the Citronella smelling variety that (supposedly) is a deterrent to the pesky mosquito.

Another favorite is mint and, again, this popular scent is available in any number of species of plant life. The peppermint plant is quite often grown outside a backdoor just to get wafts into the house when gentle breezes carry it in that direction. Many cooks use the foliage for flavoring and the leaves quite often are harvested to prepare mint tea. Spearmint is yet another of the mint family.

Goshen used to have their own peppermint farm east of town on SR 4 in the flat muck grounds where it was grown commercially to extract the oils from the plant. It was in great demand for its use in gum, perfumes, and soaps and this bottom ground was the perfect soil. There had been a shed standing in the field for many years that was part of the operation.

The ever-popular "scented" geranium is available in numerous scents and is quite easy to grow. My picks while a garden center mgr., and seemingly the customers favorites also, were the scents of rose, apricot, pineapple, apple, lemon, and chocolate mint.

Herbs present yet another aspect to growing for scent but herbs are also grown for their floral displays as well. Since we're discussing plant scent, rather than floral scent, I'll give examples because of the plant scent and uses:

Sweet Basil is far and away the most popular in this category because of its many uses in flavoring soups, meats, and all kinds of dishes.
Chervil — primarily used in soups, salads, and sauces.
Chives — used for a subtle onion-like flavor in salads and soups
Dill — used to flavor pickles and beets.
Fennel — adds an anise flavor — watch them carefully because aphids love them.
Lavender — mostly used for fragrance in sachets.
Lovage — used in soups and salads for a celery flavor.
Oregano — use it on pizza or in Italian sauces.
Rosemary — flavors a meat dish.
Summer Savory — best used as a condiment with meats and vegetables.
Thyme — is great in a gumbo or in poultry stuffing.

GIVE A CHILD THE GIFT OF GARDENING

Children are always curious about nature. What better way to introduce them to a lifetime of enjoyment than to teach them gardening by planting seeds. See them watch with amazement and excitement as the growth cycles of their living plants evolve and turn into mature healthy specimens. That first thrust of a plant poking its nose up through the soil from a seed that they have planted, tended to, and watered for several weeks is an enormous sense of achievement for a fledging gardener. Take it a step farther and use several varieties of plant seeds that compliment each other for color, for size, and for height and so on. This can be accomplished outdoors, when weather permits, or simply in a container, large or small, that is started inside. Let them get their hands dirty and have some fun.

School teachers made it a yearly event for a class to visit the greenhouse that I managed just to see plants in various stages of growth and color. Each year we gave every student a small pot filled with growing medium and several seeds that they could take back to the class room and plant. I thought this was really neat that a teacher would march the class to the greenhouses and allow them to participate in a growing symposium. I guess teaching isn't totally in books but in real life experiences too.

When I was a youngster in school at Middlebury it was Balyeat's Greenhouse that we visited just a short distance from the school on Main Street. I can still remember all the red Geraniums that Byron raised and sold. It was a brisk business and one of the only ones around that still had the "glass" greenhouses.

Nowadays greenhouses are nearly all plastic covered arches or the newer honeycomb clear plastic paneled buildings and are dotted throughout the countryside — many as a supplementary income for farmers — a few have grown to be quite large. They all have their niches and specialties and compliment each other with the many varieties they have to offer. One needs to look no farther than their local newspaper for a half dozen or more. Of course there are the handful of area nursery and greenhouse operations that have been doing business for decades that offer every kind of service there is and are a year-round business. Recently big box stores have entered the fray with mega displays of merchandise to entice the public.

The next time you take a trip to one of these "oases", take the younger school-aged children along to observe and learn about the many plant varieties that they can help plant. Supervision is suggested because of the delicacy of some of the plants but kids learn early this way about the do's and the don'ts when handling plants. It will give them a sense of helping to contribute in the family garden by allowing them to plant and learn.

EVERY GARDENER WAS A BEGINNER

True, every gardener was a beginner at some point in time and knowledge grows from that point by repetition, reading, or help from a more knowledgeable and experienced friend or acquaintance. This article is primarily for the first time gardener or for the less seasoned gardener that wants to find out the do's and don'ts and the most common faults in everyday gardening.

Growing a garden isn't "rocket science" but knowing common mistakes can lead to a healthier and thriving patch of land that gives back — not only by the fresh fruits, vegetables, and herbs it produces but also by the self-satisfaction it gives the individual and the re-assurance of "I can do that".

In creating a location for your garden consider these facts: does it receive a minimum of six hours of sunlight daily (more is better) and is its location in a convenient spot that you will have easy access to a water source and handy enough for daily grooming duties.

Once the location is determined decide whether you want a standard plowed or cultivated area or if you might want to try a raised bed garden. Raised beds are becoming more popular in recent years, especially in more confined city lots, because of their neatness in appearance and the fact that they can be placed right next to a back door, deck, or patio and fit right in with other plantings.

The next most important part is soil because it is a crucial part of your growing experience and has the ability to "make or break" any garden. A good loamy soil that has the proper nutrients in it will grow healthy bumper crops instead of failed seeds and plants or stunted crops that don't live up to their name. If you don't have the proper healthy soil, then plan on adding fertilizer, compost, and/or some additional black top-soil to "beef it up".

In a raised bed that is six inches higher than ground level add 40 % black dirt, 40% organic peat, and 20% organic cow manure and cultivate in with existing ground soil to a depth of twelve inches. A raised bed can be created by arranging landscape timbers two high, overlapped at the corners , and nailed with landscape nails or with 2X6's or 2X8's, nailed at the corners — preferably treated lumber that will not rot.

If you're lucky enough to find some mushroom mulch at a garden center then work two or three inches into the bed as a "topper"- it's gold in your garden. It had been sold bulk in our area but since Campbell's Mushroom Farm left our area it's harder to find.

Now that your garden is prepared, the search for seeds and/or plants at your local garden centers starts. Seeds will give you a much broader range of choices but plants give you a head start. If seeds are your choice, it's wise to start them indoors in a soil-less potting mix that is made up of primarily ground wood bark and peat with added booster ingredients including a charge of fertilizer. Miracle-Gro Potting Soil is a tried and true example.

Keep your pots or trays in a sunny location to prevent plants from getting "leggy". Plan when to start by the label on the seed package — it will give you the time to maturity — simply work backwards from the time you want to plant them and you'll know when to start. Keep your plants moist but take care not to overwater — this could cause what is referred to as "damping off"- a rotting at the base of the plant that will cause the plant to die — (also known as starting over).

Probably the most common fault of a beginner is not allowing enough space for plants to mature. A plant looks lonely in a garden but always check for the size at maturity. I've done it (and most have too) crowded plants together that eventually suffocate surrounding plants and making it nearly impossible to harvest anything because you can't see or find the finished product. A good example of this is a Zucchini plant that requires a great deal of space to mature. You can control this to a degree (especially in a smaller raised bed) by going up rather than out. This works especially well for cucumbers by forming a six foot piece of fencing into a circle and securing with wire. Place the cylinder over the mounded cluster of three plants and secure by weaving dowels or long sticks thru the fencing and into the soil. If you have several of these towers secure them all together. You've saved an enormous amount of space and make harvesting much easier. Beans are another example of crowding. A frame resembling a tent that has been strung with cord for the climbers to wind on is a simple solution to an otherwise nightmare of tangled masses. Of course you can always resort to the bush variety. The name of the game is planning.

Another common fault is neglect — good intentions gone haywire. Gardens take time and toil because they become dry and need to be watered, they need constant weeding, they need to be protected from common diseases and insects, and they will benefit from fertilization and of course need to be harvested regularly.

All this may sound like a lot to take on but trust me, the rewards will far exceed the effort and once your garden is established you'll find it easier each following year. It is a lesson in self-sufficiency and in these times we can all use some of that.

SPRING LIVING

Nothing says 'spring' more than that first step outside on a balmy morning and that breathe of moist, warmer than usual, air in your nostrils. It's a pick-me-up after the cold harsh days of winter and it gives everyone a spring in their step and a spurt of energy that was lost since the doldrums of fall clean-up of the preceding year.

When asked of a gardener what their favorite season is, it nearly always is spring and there's good reason. It's an awakening of nature — when trees and plants spring to life and start their journey of regeneration.

Gardeners are one of the most enthusiastic members of society. They can't wait to get outside and plant something — anything! They want to see something grow.

It might be a throwback to when they were growing up and most parents had large gardens. Curiosity was in watching seeds planted and several days later seeing a plant start to emerge where each seed was placed. As I've said before -teaching a child the miracle of gardening, from the tilling of the earth to the placement of seeds to the growth of the plant and finally the blooms or the harvest, whichever the case may be, is a lifetime learning experience. They'll carry these remembrances for the rest of their lives which is a good thing. It provides one with healthy exercise, peace of mind, serenity, and achievement.

I'm always amazed at how many individuals whom one might never think of as picking up a spade or trowel are found out to be avid gardeners. The judge, the lawyer, the professor, the construction worker, and on and on spend time in the garden quite probably to relax from pressures at their workplace. Read the obituaries — they too, often have an inclusion in them of 'being an avid gardener' to the surprise of many.

Gardening is a journey that evolves from practice, research, advice, and mistakes. Each experience will enhance your knowledge and improve your skills — some may even take it to yet another level and become a Master Gardener, Master Naturalist, or Master Forester.

Gardening should be fun — whether it's to beautify, to satisfy a family's needs, or even to build a business to supplement income.

Farmer's Markets are a great source to witness the hard toils of many a gardener that beams with pride when showing off their prize crops of fruits and vegetables. Their satisfaction is derived from not only the hard work from their gardens to the market but also the feedback from satisfied customers that return each week with compliments and praise.

Procrastinate no more — spring is here and flower and vegetable plants are arriving at garden centers throughout the area and growers and retailers are eager to help and lend you their expertise and knowledge.

I hear the buzz from some locals that they are planning to increase their vegetable garden space to help reduce the shock of the increasing costs of living. If space allows this, then why not grow a little extra? You might have a family member, a friend, or a neighbor that would welcome having fresh 'garden grown' veggies — even trade different or unusual varieties.

Space becomes a major factor (especially in city lots) and consequently crowding is the demon that causes failure. I too became guilty of this problem because I was always trying to raise too many things in too small a space. To overcome this I limited my space to fewer varieties and went taller. I built cylinders for my cucumbers to grow on, tied my tomatoes with green plastic gardener's tape to a six foot tall framework built out of 2X2's, and constructed a tent shaped trellis that I strung binder twine on for my string beans. This, along with some of the smaller green onions and green peppers was all done in an 8' X 16' raised bed garden. I even saved space for a couple of zucchini plants. Probably not the most handsome of gardens but it worked well.

Always remember to allow enough space for growth and sun and air — if plants don't receive an adequate amount of sunshine, (6 to 8 hours a day) with good circulation throughout, then they won't develop and ripen naturally.

Tomatoes are common in most every garden from the old fashion varieties like Rutgers and Beefsteak to the more recently developed Big Boy, Big Girl, and Better Boy. Cherry tomatoes are yet another hit, reference the Sweet 100, grape, and the yellow pear.

They are relatively easy to grow which makes them a favorite, however, they too can become a problem and not develop like planned. Unwanted cracking of the fruit is caused by uneven watering practices — hence water them on a regular schedule. Try not to over-water but at the same time don't under-water.

Another common problem with tomatoes is blight, when foliage yellows and drops. This is problematic and can only be corrected with proper practices. Spores develop causing spotting and yellowing on vegetation and are splashed to the soil surface. Each watering splashes more of the spores to the plants. The only way to overcome this is to remove the infested leaves and the surface of the soil. Spray with a fungicide and replace the removed soil with fresh soil or mulch. Rotate planting the following year by planting your tomatoes in a different location if possible.

Crocuses are flourishing everywhere with daffodils and tulips right on their heels — a precursor of what's to come — it's Spring!

FLOWER GARDENING

THE QUIRKY AND UNUSUAL BOTTLEBRUSH PLANT

There are numerous plants that have that familiar bottlebrush look as a flower but only one that is actually named Bottlebrush plant. It gets its name from its flower head resembling that all-too-familiar kitchen gadget that we use to get into a 'too small for the hand' opening like a thermos or a small necked vase or bottle.

To name a few of the others, there is the familiar Butterfly bush with its pendulum arching flower head, the potted Chenille that has the wooly worm looking pink/orange blossoms that is normally found as a hanging basket, and another not-so-familiar, but a prized landscape shrub, called Fothergilla 'Mount Airy' that displays a white bottlebrush and is even more valuable for its brilliant fall display of rust/bronze/orange colored leaves.

The Bottlebrush plant (Callistemon) is quite common in Phoenix and known there as Red Bottlebrush or Little John and is considered evergreen with dark green foliage. They prefer the desert southwest because they are nearly drought resistant and can handle the dry conditions of the desert. When placed in a landscape setting in dry climates, however, it will benefit from a drip-line placed near the base as a water source.

Flowering occurs in the spring to mid-summer but the shrub itself remains as a low growing dwarf reaching a height of only two feet or so. One might occasionally see them in a tree form growing ten to twelve feet tall but as a domesticated shrub they are normally sold in this dwarf version. The flower-heads, normally red in color but sometimes pink, yellow or even white, attract hummingbirds as well as other nectar loving insects.

They originated in the more temperate coastal regions of Australia and favored moist conditions so when planted in gardens there they thrived with regular watering practices, however, the cultivar we are familiar with in the states is a drought resistant strain and more conducive to dry climates.

While the Bottlebrush plant is an interesting and unusual landscape inclusion it probably is more suited for the southern and dryer states. A more acceptable shrub for our area that has a somewhat same appearance might be the Fothergilla 'Mt. Airy'.

At the garden center we had several requests for this plant so we did what we always did — we ordered it and made several people very happy.

That's what made this job so interesting because I had never heard of the Fothergilla plant so I got an education as well. If you are lucky enough to find one it would make a handsome inclusion to any landscape whether it is a foundation inclusion or in a garden bed. While not the easiest to gain a firm footing, with a little TLC they should establish themselves. Height and width are in the four to five foot range and they will thrive in an acidic moist soil with full sun or partial shade.

FORCING BULBS TO BLOOM EARLY

Wouldn't it be nice to have colorful spring blooms in the dead of winter? You can make it happen and it's easier than one might think.

Garden centers and the 'Big Box' stores more than likely still have bulbs for sale and quite often they're eager to get rid of what is left over, from fall merchandise, with year-end sales.

In fact, it's not too late to plant bulbs for spring blooms in your garden as long as you can still work the soil. Planting can continue even into December if the soil hasn't frozen hard.

Holland bulbs are usually packaged in convenient sized packages of 10 or 12 for Tulips and Daffodils and 5 or 6 for the larger Hyacinth bulbs. Crocus, Paper-whites, and Grape Hyacinths normally will be packaged in higher quantities basically because of their smaller size.

Common practice when planting bulbs is to "scatter" the bulbs to create a more natural sequence of placement rather than to create rows, however, sometimes it just isn't practical and a row or rows have to suffice. If it has to be in rows then offset each row in a zigzag pattern.

Always plant bulbs to a depth of at least twice their height — Tulips and Daffodils will do better if planted a depth of even three times their height.

Allium bulbs, because of their size (3 to 4 inches in diameter) are normally sold individually. They can be quite expensive to purchase, especially in quantities, but their statement is like no other with massive four and five inch globes of purple, blue, or white atop strong two to four foot tubular spikes. Plant them in clusters for a blast of color or they will make a formal statement when planted evenly in front of a split-rail fence.

Smaller bulbs like Paper-whites and crocus may be scattered in a garden or even thrown in the lawn and planted — they'll peek through the grass blades in the spring and welcome you with early spring color.

Now then — for color inside your home in the middle of the winter doldrums, plant Tulips, Hyacinth, and Daffodils (Jonquils) in shallow two to four inch depth containers. Use a planting medium like an all-purpose potting soil or (my favorite) "Miracle Gro" potting soil. A shallow clay pot (a glazed and colored exterior finish adds sparkle) eight to twelve inches in diameter will suffice.

These 'forced' bulbs don't have to be planted to a normal depth and may even be left with the bulb tops exposed. Arrange them in a pleasing pattern and remove to a cold and dark spot after a moderate drink and enclosing in a paper bag or a box. A refrigerator will work but only if there are no other fruits and vegetables stored in it and the pot can be enclosed and blocked of any light what-so-ever. Your achievement is to develop root structures with no foliage.

After six to eight weeks in solitary confinement they may be removed to a bright and sunny location. It shouldn't take long in the new warm atmosphere and a warm drink for them to spring forth with green foliage. Turn the pot frequently to prevent 'leaning' and before you know it there will be a blast of color and the sweet smell of spring. Give it a try — it's easy and fun!

QUILT PATTERN GARDENS

Quilt pattern gardens are an expression of one's artistic talents and abilities with the use of vegetation and gardening skills as a canvas. They have become symbols and beacons to draw attention to and attract the visiting public to retailers and city parks everywhere.

I'm not certain where it all began but I'd like to think it started in the Elkhart and LaGrange County area in Indiana.

They have emerged from simple beginnings in which there was a square with two or three colors that blended well to huge and exact replicas of famous quilts that we might see displayed at the Mennonite Relief Auction and many other retail locations throughout our northern counties or they may be the result of someone's creative imagination brought to fruition.

I must say, the creativity I've seen all over our northern counties amazes me not only with the richness of the colors but also the refinement of the patterns with crisp edges to exemplify the images. The designs themselves may be the creation of a talented artist or possibly several working together but the actual physical replication is usually by the sweat and brow of many workers. The follow-up work, after the initial planting, of weeding and more weeding is what we gardeners like to refer to as "love of garden-ing".

One's imagination can run wild when designing a pattern for a quilt gar-den — even the inclusion of grassed area divider strips such as at The Old Bag Factory.

Not only do colors and harmonizing come into play when designing a pattern but also the consideration of varying heights at maturity of the many plants involved. One can only dream and wait at what might show up next year — I'm sure it will be even more impressive.

I was especially impressed by a display last year (2011) at the Krider Park in Middlebury that displayed a sunburst pattern that had the same pattern replicated on several benches throughout the park. I'm not sure which came first, the bench or the garden for the theme (the old "which came first theory — the chicken or the egg"), but it was one of those special "oh my" moments — needless to say, my camera was clicking!

I for one would like to know, at each location, who the designer/artist is and the group sponsoring or attributing to the project — may be something to consider in future gardens by means of a small sign — I'm sure I'm not the only curious person. An artist thrives on notoriety and groups deserve the special recognition for their hard work. It may be that I've simply over-looked it in my excitement.

Hopefully the trend continues with new and even more impressive dis-plays next year — I can't get enough of them. I think the planners and de-signers are having more fun than the observers, if that is even possible.

A special thanks to the 'keepers' of the gardens who had to overcome the heat and draught of this unusual year. It took great perseverance to keep these beautiful gardens in pristine condition — no small task.

Fall garden color is always a challenge and if you've ever wondered what that beautiful purple shrub in bloom this time of year is, it's none other than Caryopteris or better known as Blue Mist Shrub- a late bloomer that will brighten the landscape with a luminous blue.

PETUNIA — THE MOST STAPLE ANNUAL IN YOUR GARDEN

I've often been asked "what is the best flower to plant in full sun that will give me the least amount of grief" and my answer, without hesitation, is always petunias.

Petunias have that unique ability to thrive in just about any type of weather, even in less than ideal spots, and be it full sun or partial shade, thrive with the least amount of care. This is not to say they don't have preferences because they do — ideally they like full sun and somewhat dry conditions to develop happily.

When wet weather is in abundance they droop, until completely dry again, and once dry they say thank you for the drink and spring forth happily again. In fact keep watering practices to a minimum, keeping the soil on the dry side, and when watering (if at all practical) lift to water only the dirt and not the foliage and blossoms.

Cities that have container baskets hanging from light posts nearly always use petunias as the dominate flower and even if other plants are included it's usually the petunia that thrives and eventually takes over the entire basket. This happens because they like dry and when baskets might not get watered on a regular basis they will still perform nicely. Most cities, however, will have a 'caretaker' that makes the rounds regularly with water and fertilizer to keep them looking their best — some are amazingly beautiful.

Each year representatives of the professional horticultural industry select one flower, one vegetable, and one perennial to be showcased. Each is chosen because they are popular, easy to grow, widely adaptable, genetically diverse, and versatile. In 1997 the petunia was chosen "Year of the Petunia".

It has been proclaimed to be, without doubt, one of the most popular flowers ever to grace our gardens, porches, and patios. They will edge a flower bed or may be used as a groundcover or used in a container on a rail to spill out over the edge and flow as a cascading waterfall. Their performance through the season from spring until fall takes a back seat to none.

Petunias originated in South America back in the 1700's and 1800's and brought to Europe in the 1800's. They were a far cry from our present-day variety having much smaller blossoms and lanky in appearance. Breeders in Germany and England began crossing them in search of larger flowers and more colors – the originals were white or purple flowered only. They were successful in their venture and hybridized them into many exciting new colors, some with fringed edges and even some doubles.

Hybridizing continued again in the 50's after World War II and the first true red was developed and tagged "Comanche" which to this day I remember as a 'red-hot' seller at our store in Middlebury, Indiana then came the first true yellow (Summer Sun) in 1977. In more recent years (1995) the Purple Wave series was introduced as an AAS Winner (All American Selection) that began a whole new class of spreading petunias, leading to changes that completely transformed the garden petunia as we know it. This happened shortly after I took over the management at Everett's Garden Center — it was difficult keeping up with all the new entries into the market but it made for some exciting times with customer's demands for all the newest and latest varieties.

There are in this species: Grandiflora, Multiflora, Spreading, Floribunda, and even Milliflora (a new class of petunias named 'Fantasy' introduced in 1996). The Milliflora was hybridized to produce a smaller but more prolific bloomer with blossoms reaching only 1 to 1 ½ inches across but their branching habit is contained to be perfect for hanging baskets.

They will benefit from a regular fertilizing program (every 2 to 3 weeks) but should be watered sparingly (at the wilt stage) unless planted in containers where they should be observed daily for dryness.

THINGS ARE NOT ALWAYS AS THEY APPEAR TO BE

A beautiful flower — or is it? One can't always believe what their eyes tell them. At first glance you'd say "what is this magnificent specimen of flower growing next to my tree"? But wait — this 'flower' measures a full twelve inches in diameter — now that would be a BIG blossom! There are a few that could rival that, like the dinner-plate size Hibiscus blossoms, but this one had unusual properties as well.

It is like no other I had ever seen as its brilliant orange (near fluorescent) petals stood out magnificently, only to be overshadowed by the even more brilliant yellow fringe edging each petal displayed.

Believe it or not this 'flower' is none other than a fungus growing next to and on a tree in north Goshen.

It was brought to my attention by a devoted reader of my column and thought it would be an interesting subject and topic — she too had never seen anything like it before.

The owners have lived in the same home for the past 37 years and are avid gardeners, especially since retirement, on their sprawling five acre tract that consumes a good deal of time in just mowing chores. A large pond at the rear of their property helps to alleviate some of the mowing and some is left 'wild' as a natural habitat.

I could see a lot of 'old school' and tradition in my visit with a, larger than most, vegetable garden that supplies them with a constant source of fresh vegetables throughout the growing season.

My wife and I have known the family since the seventies as we both had daughters growing up together and there would be many 'sleep-overs' at both places. Our daughter and the family's daughter were always good buddies while growing up and there was usually a gang of six or eight that always 'hung out'.

Thank you for the invite and the unusual topic.

I receive quite a number of calls with the usual "are you the Tom Yoder that writes the gardening column for The Goshen News? When not at home they'll leave a message and I try to respond to as many as I can (if name and number are included) because nearly all have 'new or unusual' topics that I'm sure everyone who is a gardener would find as interesting a subject as I do.

A lot of my columns are because of phone calls such as this or when I'm out and about and run into people that recognize or know me. My wife too gets the "You're Tom Yoder's wife who writes the gardening column for The Goshen News, aren't you?" She smiles and happily acknowledges the recognition.

IF YOU WANT DEPENDABLE THEN THIS IS YOUR PLANT

Double Early Sunrise Coreopsis is probably one of the most dependable plants that you can grow because they effortlessly renew your flower bed with a burst of sunny yellow each year.

They are easily propagated by seed or by cuttings and quite often spread to surrounding areas simply by birds, ground animals , and even wind, but not to worry because they are easily eliminated by simply removing them along with your normal weeding. If so desired, the removed seedlings may be transplanted to other areas with nearly 100% success.

At Everett's Garden Center we planted several clumps along the fence row in front of the business and each year they would spring forth in all their glory to give customers a first-hand glimpse of what to expect when planted in their own garden. These along with Purple Coneflower, also planted in the fence row, made quite a statement to patrons visiting the garden center.

The nice thing about Coreopsis of all kinds (and there are many) is the continuous blooming from mid-May into and through September. Some perform a little better than others but for the most part I think you'll be happy with the performance of them all.

Early Sunrise, double or the single petal variety, is probably the best for continuous day to day blooming. Simply remove the spent blooms and more blooms will follow.

Coreopsis Tequila Sunrise is another noted for their continuous blooming and it too spreads nicely. Another plus is even though they spread quite easily they are not considered invasive. Foliage of this species has a cream border tinged in pink that encircles a green leaf.

Coreopsis, commonly called tickseed, is known for its burnt orange or red eye that strikes quite a nice color combination with the brilliant yellow/orange of the petals. Another plus is that they thrive in less than ideal soil conditions and have a profuse blooming reputation.

They can readily be seen along roadways intertwined with another favorite, Blue Flax (also drought resistant), creating a rural spectacle on country roads. Some consider Blue Flax a wildflower but it has been domesticated and can readily be found at garden centers everywhere.

Moonbeam Coreopsis is yet another of this wonderful family. It is my favorite not only because of the delicate pure yellow blossoms but also the fine grass-like foliage of this one-of-a-kind plant. It grows in a mounded shape approximately two feet in height with a spread of two to three feet and blooms continuously through the summer months. Like many other perennials, however, the early flush is the most prolific waning somewhat through the rest of the season. After that first flush has diminished some prefer to cut it back for another full burst of color later in the season. There is nothing much prettier than several clumps of this with a backdrop of several clumps of Russian Sage. Wow!

There are several other of this species worth mentioning one of which is a rose colored Moonbeam Coreopsis although its prolificacy is not nearly what the yellow is. Some others are Mercury Rising, a velvet wine color with a mahogany center; Coreopsis Redshift, a butter yellow with a crimson eye; Coreopsis Tweety, known for its brilliant yellow (comparable to Moonbeam) with a somewhat dwarf habit of 14"-16" in height and 10"- 14" of spread with color May thru September; Zagreb Coreopsis is another similar to Moonbeam but somewhat taller on stiffer stems and slightly less prolific with their blossoming.

GET YOUR BLOOM ON

Perennials all have their blooming periods, some just more than others. While the usual flush of blossoms for perennials is about four to six weeks, there are a few that will perform eight to twelve weeks on average.

Planning perennial gardens is always a challenge because we want to have continuous blooming from at least May through August. It can be accomplished but it takes a considerable amount of research to find species that will burst into color when others are fading away. Not only are we looking for continuity but also complimentary colors that look good with each other.

Once the bloom periods are established and the colors blend with their surrounding counterparts we have the anchors, so to speak, of a perennial garden and then minor inclusions of an unusual plant for a spot of color or other annuals, to incorporate a border, can give it that 'finished' look.

While it is often difficult for the average gardener to restrain themselves (me included) from planting everything and every color in the same bed it would be wise to keep beds to a maximum of two or three colors at most — there's something to be said about too many focal points in any 'one' garden just as in art where a single focal point is preferred. This can be overcome by having several gardens with differing color combinations.

Like the experts always say, "less is more"- it prevents the eye from 'bouncing' and makes it easier to focus.

What's blooming now? As far as perennials go, Rudbeckia (Black-eyed Susan) and Echinacea (Coneflower) are in their prime at this writing and they are two of the longest lasting perennials that I know of. They will make a good pair in a bed and can be expected to bloom from June through August. A bed of these two outstanding performers with the inclusion of a spot highlight like Russian Sage or a tall grass may be all that is necessary for a home's focal point. Add a complimentary border of a contrasting color and there you have it!

Other plants that are in bloom at this writing (however with shorter life spans) are gladiola and daylilies.

Gladiolas are excellent for cut flower arrangements. They came into season in lower Michigan about the same time that peaches and apples were starting so I would always have to pick up several dozen of cut bunches each with four or five single stems of like color and variety. They were always welcomed by the fruit shoppers and hard to resist.

If you want a daylily that will perform continuously for many weeks try Stella 'de Oro — it has outstanding lasting qualities and a longer than usual bloom period. When blooms wane be sure to snip stems back as far into the plant as can be reached. Another hint is to reach into its depths and yank out dead and old growth — it seems to rejuvenate the plant to continue and extend its bloom period.

CLEMATIS WILL PUT ON AN IMPRESSIVE DISPLAY

There's no missing clematis when in full bloom and in all their glory. They are visible from a great distance, especially when growing on a trellis or support. Fully developed examples that have had several years to mature will surprise most gardeners with huge canopies of blossoms.

The variety Jackmanii with its deep purple velvet blooms are far and away the most popular because of its prolificacy that will easily create a focal point in any garden setting.

There are two great specimens of Jackmanii that dominate each corner of a fenced backyard adjacent to a cart path by the number eleven green at the Black Squirrel Golf Course in Goshen. I pass there often and admire them each time I pass — so beautiful.

When driving down a country road it's not unusual to see a clematis planted at a mailbox to give color and to conceal the post or even a rail fence with a clematis trailing along its rails giving it a lineal line of color — planted no doubt by an avid gardener to please themselves but also to add eye candy to every passerby.

Mine occupied the northeast corner of my home. I had built a trellis for it to climb on out of a 2'X8' piece of lattice and painted it white. This was mounted on a 4"X4" treated post that I buried in the ground a couple feet. When in full bloom it covered four of the eight feet with the top billowing downward in a three foot wide spectacle. Many who saw it couldn't believe the size but this was another case of it liking where it was planted. It captured the full sun at its top with shade at its feet.

It was shaded with a groundcover and for the most part continuously shaded from direct sun at its base so that moisture was always present — (important to clematis). Also, with a groundcover you aren't disturbing the roots (equally important to clematis) as their roots rise very close to the surface to capture much needed moisture to support its canopy.

Some may choose other varieties that are also popular on the market to have two or several colors that blend well together. My next favorite would be Nellie Moser, a beauty which is pink with mauve colored margins that contrast well with a Jackmanii — in fact one sits at my back door since I moved to a condo.

Other longstanding popular varieties that you might want to consider include: The President (purple); Will Goodman (blue); Margaret Koster (rosy/red); Madame Le Coultre (white); Capitaine Thuileaux (strawberry pink bars on a cream background).

Paniculata (sweet autumn) is a fall variety of clematis that produces thousands and thousands of nickel size white blooms and is one of the easiest of the clematis family to grow. From a distance it appears as a cloud of white because of its robust growth habit. They will grow quite nicely on a fence or cover a walkthrough trellis because of its natural ability to entwine whatever it grows on.

I had one that occupied a corner outside my three season room that provided us with not only a spectacular sight but also a sweet floral scent when in bloom. My neighbor and friend, Sandy Drudge, had one that peeked over her low fenced backyard spilling over the top and along its length for all lookers to admire.

While I trimmed mine back to a couple feet after a hard freeze, some leave old growth to form a natural trellis for new growth to climb on the following year.

One of the drawbacks I found with the fall clematis is the continual sprouting of new starts at the base of the parent. While it is somewhat a nuisance it does provide one (if lifted and potted) with an opportunity to gift them to friends. I found it a small inconvenience in exchange for the wonderment of the plant.

TRIED AND TRUE DIANTHUS

Dianthus (aka: Carnations, Pinks, Sweet William) is a genus of about 300 species native mainly to Europe and Asia so says Wikipedia (an on-line authoritative source). The name Dianthus is derived from the Greek words dios ("god") and anthos ("flower"). The species are mostly perennial herbs with a few being annual or biennial and some are low subshrubs with woody basal stems.

The origin of the flower name 'pink' may come from the frilled edge of the flowers. The verb "pink" dates from the fourteenth century and means "to decorate with a perforated or punched pattern" (maybe from the German "pinken" — to peck.) Source: *Collins Dictionary*. The verb sense is also used in the name of pinking shears.

While most Dianthus sold in our area are considered annuals, they grow in the southern states as perennials. Pinks and Carnations grown in our area, however, are perennial and re-emerge yearly if properly cared for.

This species have some peculiarities in that they hate being overwatered and only require water in the extended absence of rain. Another is that they don't like to be mulched — simply plant at ground level in a good composted soil that leans toward acidity. They will thrive best in cooler climates but will do quite nicely in any sunny location.

If you have a rock garden (or would like to) then Dianthus are a natural inclusion, some even draping over rocky edges in a waterfall fashion.

I've always enjoyed them because of their bright blast of color. It's hard to find any annual flower (especially the annual varieties of Dianthus) that offer more bright colors and interesting color patterns than these.

If a planter or potted arrangement needed an "attention getter" then these would do the job with deep brilliant double reds, cerulean blues, and soft pinks.

Carnations and Pinks are of the same genus, are considered perennial, and their foliage is silver and frosty instead of the deep green that the annual varieties have. Carnations grow on stout (and taller) stems.

Another of the species are 'perennial' and grow in a rounded mounding shape with a fine lacy and wispy foliage and produce massive amounts of tiny flowers at the tips of each appendage. This creates a visual burst of color that deserves a second and third look. Like the annual varieties, they also have unmatched brilliance with the reds appearing to be on fire — hence the name "Bright Lights".

With most vegetable gardens well on their way it is always a good idea to repeat the fertilizing to give rooting plants an added boost.

Encircle tomato plants with a general purpose garden fertilizer and carefully scratch into the soil so as to not damage tender roots. The same may be done for cucumbers and zucchini plants. Rows may be side dressed by making a shallow trench, fertilizer drizzled in, re-covered, and in all cases thoroughly watered.

If you prefer, a liquid application of fertilizer (like Miracle-Gro) can be substituted for granular fertilizer but must be repeated more often to gain the same results.

THIS IS NOT A DAUNTING TASK

Want to try something different when it comes to planting? What one might consider too much effort or too difficult to even entertain a try, I say go for it.

Constructing a growing wreath is somewhat challenging but if you know the basics it becomes much more a simple task.

While you may construct one with any circular frame, I would suggest purchasing a commercial frame constructed just for this purpose. They are made of heavy wire, concave in shape, and most have a flat "lid" also of the same wire that may be snapped in place once the necessary ingredients are in place (I preferred to eliminate the lid and simply place moss on top and wire it securely). They will vary in size but the most popular are 16" to 24" in diameter.

To start, you will need sphagnum moss or Canadian sheet moss to form a tight liner in the concave form. Soak either in water for fifteen minutes to gain flexibility of the product and to provide good absorption once everything is planted for that first good soaking.

Line the concave frame with moss taking care to cover every square inch thoroughly so as to contain the medium that will be placed into it.

Second you will need a good medium like Miracle-Gro Potting Mix or similar.

While you may use the punch method by simply punching holes in the sphagnum and planting flower plugs into the contained medium, I prefer to use 4" potted plants that fit nicely into the concave shape of the circle by inserting them somewhat on their side but not so much that you can't tilt them upwards. This is all accomplished while the frame lies flat on your work bench.

Once the frame is completely filled with your plants it's time to fill any remaining holes with medium, packing somewhat tightly in and around the plants. The next step is to weave more moss on top and around the plants to eliminate any leakage of the planting medium.

The final step is to secure green floral wire to the upper edge of the frame and crisscross it back and forth over the moss and between the plants so that all is secured.

Once this final step is completed you may add smaller plugs of various complimentary plants by using the punch method by forming a small hole and inserting them securely through the moss.

It is best to leave the wreath lying flat for at least a week to allow the plants to start their rooting. Always be sure to keep them well watered and fertilized. If instructions were followed exactly and rooting and growth develops then a daily soak should suffice. The wreath may be removed from its final hanging spot to water if preferred — it is sometimes not practical to water it while hanging and better absorption is accomplished while lying flat.

Growing wreaths aren't limited to just flowers. Vines may be incorporated into the wreath and left to trail or may be woven around the circle. I've also seen some very handsome wreaths made entirely of succulents of various shapes, colors, and textures.

PLANT A MASTERPIECE IN YOUR CONTAINER

Creativity is the bastion of all gardeners and it starts with that first attempt at putting together an arrangement of different flowers in a miniature garden, i.e.: a pot, urn, or basket. Trial and error is a common practice but once one understands the growing habits of different plants — height at maturity, spread, and sun/shade preferences, then it simply boils down to color choices.

Colors run rampant, so what used to be the norm, now are being replaced with new hybrid colors that boggle the mind. Color combinations that one might never had dreamed of 'putting together' turn out to be handsome and complimentary to each other. Vast contrasts of color or subtle differences can make or break an arrangement. I've even used nothing but green leafed plants in a potted urn but the greens varied from emerald green to soft gray/green to deep hunter green and all with varying textures like flat leaves, rippled leaves, and even fine fern-like textured leaves. I've seen remarkable arrangements of only subtle differences of blue and purple or oranges or pinks.

It's an artistic adventure when one stands in front of an empty container filled only with a planting medium. Arrangement of plants on the surface can help in making your final decision before actual planting. If, after planting, something doesn't look quite right then simply lift and re-arrange. Where the final placement of the container will eventually be is also a consideration. You may want taller plants in the rear if placing next to a wall. If the grouping will stand in the open then taller plants will usually go in the middle.

When shopping for plants, what appears to be perfect companions may not be perfect in performance. In other words — watch for blooming periods and check labels for adaptability to sun or shade and check for watering and/or feeding requirements.

Shop around if you are able — there are a multitude of garden centers, big box stores, and nurseries throughout the area and what one may not have, the other may have exactly what you're looking for. Farmer owned greenhouses dot the countryside in a thirty mile radius and all are promoting their own specialties. I've been to many but certainly not all and most I've visited have been friendly and knowledgeable. Older established garden centers are dominant in and around the city and have seldom disappointed. A few specialize in mostly vegetable plants.

Word of mouth is usually the determining factor when it comes to finding that perfect one and only 'fit' that you're looking for. I heard that a lot when engaged in managing the garden center at Everett's. Customer's chatter usually revolved around "oh, I saw it at so and so" or "this is the only place that has it" or "this is the nicest I've seen". It was always reassuring when customers complimented you on the vast choices to be had.

My suppliers rarely let me down when searching for a customer's special wants — if they didn't grow it they found it via another grower and had it delivered to their place for me to pick up. Trips to the Kalamazoo area were on a daily basis as truckload after truckload were brought to the garden center with eager gardeners salivating and anxious for the doors to open to bulging shelves of beautiful plants. It made my heart swell with pride for every satisfied customer. It was an enormous amount of work that was handled in stride with all my good help.

TUBEROUS BEGONIAS YIELD BEAUTY BEYOND BELIEF

Begonias of the "tuberous" variety are a spectacle to behold — from their large hairy and textured leaves to their overall size to their spectacular colors and combinations of colors and markings. They can be classified as a succulent because of their high water content which I would guess at 95% minimum.

These beauties can be purchased at most garden center outlets as "non-stop" Begonias. Most growers grow these "non-stops" from cuttings to sell to the mass-marketers. Once purchased by the consumer they are normally kept for just one season and discarded.

Anyone can grow these if they have a spot with a northern exposure or a semi-shaded area in the landscape. They are one of the few flowering plants that keep on performing day after day in the shade or semi-shade.

If you are a dedicated gardener and have the patience, you might consider taking it to the next step and grow the crème 'de la crème of the tuberous begonias from actual tubers purchased from a nursery. These are usually sold according to size ranging from one inch to as large as three inches in diameter. These tubers (much like tulips) are rated and graded for size. Size is derived mainly by yearly increases in growth and development. In other words, generally speaking, the older the tuber the larger and costlier they will be but at the same time the larger the plant will be — sometimes reaching two feet and more in height and diameter.

Purchasing tubers will also gain you more variations in color and the combinations of color that breeders develop like the "Picotee" that I was awarded 'Best of Show' in a flower show many years ago.

It was a new introduction that year and I was excited to see it develop into the show-stopper it became — a pure white with a defined ruffled red edge standing eighteen inches in height and diameter. This coloring all happens on the female flower — yes, they have male blossoms and female blossoms — the male blossom is simply a single and white flat bloom and is, in this species, a fraction of the size of its counterpart.

If you want to try to grow tubers at home, start them in February or early March by placing them in a growing medium like "Miracle-Gro Potting Mix" or simply peat in a dark spot in the basement. A shallow tray (two inches deep) will suffice for the first step. Place tubers in the medium so that the tops are barely exposed. After two weeks and minimal moisture applied, rooting should have commenced and swelling buds should be showing. When roots are at least an inch long, transfer them to individual pots (peat pots will do) that are small enough to barely get them in without damaging the tender roots but deep enough for continued root development and also move them to more light to prevent elongation of the new top growth — root crowding is better and will help develop the plant. After the plant is somewhat root-bound, remove it then to a larger permanent pot, being careful to loosen the tight roots before re-planting.

If you are unable to find tubers at local nurseries then resort to the mail-order catalogs.

SOME FLOWERS ARE JUST MORE SPECIAL

Flowers are special — some of them more so than others. Some are so beautiful that we just can't seem to get enough of them and marvel at their perfection and colors.

One such species is the Gerbera daisy (pronounced ger-be'-re, jer-be'-re, ger- burr-ah', or jer-burr-ah'). I've heard every pronunciation and any is correct.

Never was I disappointed in my quest while searching at the large greenhouses I frequented in the Kalamazoo area (some up to 40 acres under one continuous roof). They were in abundance, and rightfully so, with large blocks of various colors of the rainbow. If you think they are amazing close up, try viewing an acre or two of them in every color.

These flowers are perfection at their best with their daisy-like flowers each a picture of pure beauty that reek with the richest colors found in any of nature's finest. Growers knew the demand and didn't disappoint — a sea of color befitting a king was at your fingertips and I couldn't resist with purchases in the thousands to satisfy our customer's demands.

I, being an artist, would find it difficult to reproduce some of the colors of this unique specimen. The purest of yellows that could imitate a sunrise, magenta and fuchsia and mauve of the red/purples that any king would be proud of, a gold so rich you might mistake it for 24 carat, a creamy white that emulates heavy cream, and a red so deep that you'd think it was bleeding — each seemingly more beautiful than the other. Placed on a 50 foot long table, most would be gone in a day or two.

Gerbera daisies are a staple at any florists as they are used quite extensively as a potted plant. As a cut flower, they have long "lasting" qualities making them ideal and suited perfectly for floral arrangements for funerals and other special events. Where color and statement are a necessary factor, you can always count on these "one of a kind".

They rank number five in popularity under the number one roses, then carnations, then chrysanthemums, and then tulips. They were named after a famous German botanist and naturalist Traugott Gerber who traveled extensively in Russia in the eighteenth century. They belong to the sunflower family.

With geranium sales, at the garden center that I managed, peaking at twenty thousand plants, Gerberas were increasingly improving their market share with sales in the thousands because of their ever increasing popularity. Geraniums still hold their number one ranking though because of their versatility and functionality. Geraniums too, take minimum upkeep other than fertilizing, watering, and dead-heading while Gerberas require a little more loving care and knowledge when it comes to how much or how little to water and just how much heat they can tolerate (they prefer cooler)-place them in a semi-shaded spot and keep them moist and they'll keep on giving.

PONDER THIS THOUGHT

God gave us the gifts of sight, smell, touch, and taste — all are traits that every gardener tries to incorporate into their gardens whether they realize it or not. This is why gardening is so ingrained in every individual who loves to work the soil. No one trait is dominant however- they all work together encompassing the whole.

Think about the color of your most beautiful rose. As magnificent as it is, it is even more beautiful because of its smell. Now touch it and feel its softness and form.

Pluck a Nasturtium flower from the vine and marvel over its brilliant yellow, orange, or red color. Now taste it — chew it like lettuce and mull its peppery taste — even the smaller tender leaves are edible. Some chefs include both the flowers and the leaves in a salad to give them a spicy, peppery taste departing from the ordinary.

Snap a fully developed bell pepper from the stalk — whether it's the deep kelly green or one of its sister varieties — chocolate brown, cherry red, or golden yellow — they all have that unique taste that only a bell pepper has. Feel its smooth skin and its bell shape and its crisp snap when pulled and bent.

Marvel over a cluster of cerulean blue Lavender in the garden — beautiful in its own right but even more so because of the pungent but delicate fragrance that wafts in the breeze.

Yank eight or ten fresh tender green onions from the soil — hose them with a fine spray of water and just the sight of them emits freshness. There's something about a fist-full of these "one of a kind taste" that says flavor. Every salad would benefit with the inclusion of these.

Sweet basil should be a natural in every garden because of its versatility. While color is not the dominant factor in this case (although the curly purple variety is quite impressive), the smell and taste abound making it a natural inclusion in many recipes, from soups to salads to a flavor enhancer for meat dishes of all kinds.

Even a freshly dug potato, each variety having their own unique shape and color, all have the same musky scent when first cut.

A Hyacinth pushing up from the soil in early spring puts on its miraculous show with a cluster of waxy florets on a stiff stem in colors rivaling a spectrum only to be outdone by the fragrance that almost overwhelms everything. Some with allergies may even be overcome by the strong perfumes emitted from them.

All, and each with their own attractions, perform their miracles in the garden and this is my point: sight is the miracle of colors and shapes; smell is the floral bouquet or the unique scent each plant, vegetable, or herb possesses; touch is the interactive feel of each blossom, garden vegetable, or even the razor sharp jagged edge of a yucca plant; taste is the tantalizing zing of an onion, radish, or tomato, and the edible flowers that are incredibly tasty or the many herbs that every discriminating gardener possesses and grows.

Gardening is a life support system that gives a special meaning to sight, smell, touch, and taste — get involved, you'll never look back.

IS THIS THE BEAUTY OR THE BEAST?

I first knew it as Canadian Lythrum when early in my married life I purchased this beautiful tall and spiky purplish/pink perennial that fit perfect in the back row of my flower bed. I admired it year after year and it soon became a favorite because of its continuous long-lasting blooming qualities. Every gardener has a flower or two that they can count on each year to be included in their flowerbeds and this plant was one of mine.

After I made my move to Goshen I tried again to find Canadian Lythrum (salicaria) to include in my new west-side flower beds. It wasn't until I began my Garden Center manager's position and dealing with growers in Michigan that I discovered why it is no longer marketed and sold in the area.

My prized perennial is also known as Purple Loosestrife which is banned in at least twenty-four states prohibiting its importation or distribution because of its aggressively invasive characteristics.

Many may not realize the invasiveness of this plant — it will eventually crowd out most other plants and vegetation and threaten an imbalance in our fragile ecosystem especially in marshlands and bogs where it will spread rapidly.

This plant doesn't send roots laterally, but rather, it branches laterally above the surface with many tendrils while choking out any plants that compete for space. It is capable of rooting from these tendrils wherever it can get a foothold to soil.

Removing this voracious grower is hardly a layman's task once it gets a foothold. If you have it on your property and it is only spotty it would be recommended that you try to remove it but if it has already spread an entire area it would be almost impossible to control. There is no known remedy to date to stifle its growth.

If an attempt is made to remove small spotty growth and plants have already started to brown at season end, first carefully place a plastic bag over the seed producing flower-head and secure it tightly around the stem. Bend the stem downward to catch all the seeds. Carefully cut the flower-head off with a pruning shears and incinerate the bag or place it in the trash to be removed to a land-fill. Don't place this in your compost pile where birds and critters can easily carry the tiny seeds on their bodies to germinate elsewhere. These tiny seeds can lay dormant for years only to raise their ugly heads later on and start anew.

Each mature plant contains two million and more of tiny sand size seeds that must be disposed of properly to avoid re-introducing them into our fragile ecosystem.

First introduced to the northeastern states from Europe in the early 1800's as a perennial garden flower, it has invaded many states by water, animals, birds, boats, and humans and is slowly becoming a threat to overtake wetland areas and stream margins everywhere.

If you're not familiar with Purple Loosestrife you may have thought it to be just another beautiful sea of purple in wetlands, however, as beautiful as it is its damage can be long lasting. The introduction of a natural predator is being considered that feeds on the leaves of the plant thus reducing the growth pattern and limiting its growth and voracity. Europe has this already that naturally controls it.

QUEEN ANNE'S LACE — A WEED, A NUISANCE, OR A FLOWER?

Well, you might say it's all three. To a farmer it's a weed and a nuisance — to the average person it's a weed but a pretty flower — to a kid it's a flower with a potential to be more than what it is in the field by coloring it red, blue, green, or yellow with food color dyes.

Many kids have observed this transformation in a classroom experiment or by a parent simply teaching them about nature and science.

There are teachers that have their classes experiment with the absorption/dying process by using various colors of food coloring in a small amount of water to be absorbed up into the flower head. It's an amazing process that turns ordinary white into an array of pastel colors. Don't stop with the usual red, green, yellow, and blue — take it another step and mix the colors. Red and yellow will make orange, blue and red will make purple, all four basics colors will result in brown. Just remember to take precautions by using a garbage bag with a hole cut out to slip over your head to avoid accidental splashes on clothing. Food coloring is not the easiest thing to get out of material. This same process is used by many florists to change Carnations from white to pastel colors to include in their arrangements.

Its botanical name, Daucus carota, is native to the temperate regions of Europe and southwest Asia. It was brought to North America where it has become naturalized in the Northeast. Our common domesticated carrots are actually cultivars of a sub-species of this plant. The roots of Queen Anne 's Lace may be eaten just like a carrot but only when they are young as they quickly become fibrous and woody as they mature.

Common names for this weed may include wild carrot, bird's nest, bishop's lace, and in the U.S. Queen Anne's Lace where they are usually seen in dry fields, ditches, and open areas. The USDA has listed it as a noxious weed and it is considered a pest in pastures by farmers who have to deal with it on a yearly basis. Many consider it an invasive weed crowding out and competing with native plants.

The flower itself resembles lace and the tiny red flower in the center represents a droplet of blood where Queen Anne pricked herself when making the lace. This red "droplet" attracts insects to the plant thus guaranteeing its reproduction.

It, being a biennial, will see the first year's growth mainly as vegetation and building size with blossoming the following year. Bloom period is generally June through September.

The flower heads will eventually curl inward forming a "bird's nest" appearance and fall to become a tumble-weed.

While most consider this a pest plant, some gardeners introduce it to attract insect predators. Queen Anne's Lace will first attract aphids and other small insects which then will attract the predators that will stay for the season.

June or the First of August is the most effective time to deal with and eradicate grubs in your lawn if they were a problem the previous year. Treatment before the eggs hatch will ensure best results when these little critters are in an eating frenzy. Treating in the spring will not only be useless but a drain on your wallet. Retailers will be pushing grub control earlier than this but applied too early will not only be expensive but basically useless. You must control these voracious little eaters when first hatched to eradicate next year's population. Don't apply the product just as a precaution either. Be responsible and apply only if you had a grub problem the prior year.

A DREAM COMES TRUE

This story originated way back in the mid-nineties when I was developing my backyard with gardens of a perennial/annual mix and included a pond, a raised vegetable garden, and a raised tree line shade garden.

I had always admired Wisteria with its long plumes of purple/blue so my plan included an arched trellis located at a pre-determined entryway into my backyard gardens. It was to be a grandiose arch that included a gate and 4 six by six boxed posts with an eight foot overhead rising moon-shaped design that I had observed in a magazine article.

To get a jump on my plans which I anticipated would materialize the following year, or at the latest the next year, I purchased my Wisteria that was to envelope my archway and stuck it in my flower bed to gain some growing time and maturity. Needless to say I was dumb-struck when the first year's growth sent shoots six and eight feet out interfering with care of my perennials and even my mowing. This thing was the healthiest and most robust thing I had ever seen but much to my dismay, no flowers. Thinking it was still immature and flowering would develop the following year, I simply waited. Next year brought the same results with even longer appendages and again no flowers.

Now I'm in my flower beds pruning back each and every one of these eight foot plus shoots. The Wisteria is getting quite large and, because of the heavy pruning, very dense.

In the meantime a showpiece garden shed took precedence over the trellis. Plans were sent for and construction kept me busy for a month. It was a beauty with a large paned window, double entry doors with long hand crafted hinges and I even included a window flower box.

Year three arrives and I'm still so busy at the garden center that I simply have no time to build my trellis entryway. Long story short — my trellis never came to fruition and consequently I'm still doing heavy pruning. My time-consuming job is now interfering with the final development of my arched trellis project.

Discussion began in the early 2000's of a move to a condominium community to relieve me of the toils of all my gardening and to concentrate solely on my job at the garden center. The decision was made and the move followed.

Now I didn't want to leave this monstrosity in the garden so it was decided that I ask one of our kids if they were interested. My step-daughter's husband came to the rescue — it was removed and placed in a favorable spot on their property. After several years of nothing but long shoots and its failure to blossom it was becoming a disappointment.

Remembering an article from a publication many years ago I suggested to my son-in-law to give this fix a try. The article stated that a Wisteria's failure to bloom might be corrected by a deep "cut" or two made with a spade a foot from the base of the plant. This procedure apparently fools the plant into thinking it's going to die and it produces flowers to be germinated and produce seeds so as to keep the species from extinction.

Well, to make a long story short, it worked and each succeeding year produces more glorious flowering. Isn't it great when a plan comes together! I'm glad someone made good use of it even if I didn't get to — and I still get to see "my" Wisteria in its full blooming glory.

COMING VERY SOON — HOLIDAY COLOR

No, not the white, cold, and wet variety that falls from the sky (that will be here too), but the seasonal influx of all the Poinsettias and holiday flowers that will fill all the shelves and aisles of your local retailers and garden centers.

This is a big deal for growers and retailers alike because it's the big push for the start of the holiday flower season and it is a billion dollar business.

John Roberts Poinsett served in the South Carolina and US House of Representatives in the early 1800's and studied plants in his spare time. While serving as the first US Ambassador to Mexico, he noticed the red flowers growing alongside the roads while traveling in southern Mexico and de-cided to bring them back to the states to his greenhouse. Known then as Mexican Fire Plant, it was renamed in honor of Ambassador Poinsett, for his introduction into the US and its spread in popularity as a symbol of the Christian holidays.

Poinsettias will be displayed in all sizes and colors and there are many — starting with a small single stem in four to six inch pots, ballooning to ten and twelve inch pots and larger with six bracts and more.

The small single stem Poinsettias are fine for a child's gift to their mother, father, or teacher or even centerpieces for tables or spot color at a holiday event. They normally will be less than ten dollars, maybe even closer to five dollars. Each bract increases the cost because of the length of time it takes to grow and develop them. Some of the largest ones can be quite costly. Though the common red variety is by far the most popular, re-cent fiddling with hybridizing and colors has developed many new varieties such as Candy Cane, Pink, White, Yellow, Purple, and Gold varieties. While these ventures from the traditional red are different and unusual and can be quite becoming in the right setting, I'm more of a traditionalist and pre-fer the standard red — it portrays the "holidays" and apparently I'm in the majority according to sales statistics where they outsell any other by a wide margin.

To prevent damage and premature loss of foliage, always cover before removing from the retailer and take precautions from frigid conditions in transporting to their final destination. Keep plants from drafts near a door-way or heating register and out of direct hot sunlight but keep them in an abundance of light. Water them thoroughly when dry to the touch but never leave the pot sit in water.

Cyclamens are another holiday favorite and usually can be purchased at floral shops around the area as well as garden centers and major retailers. Their blooms are unique in that they seem almost too perfect and even ap-pear as to be wax imitations. Their white, pink, purple, or red blossoms stand on stout stems several inches above lush green heart shaped leaves that often are a mixture of green and silver. They make perfect gifts or cen-terpieces because of their lasting qualities and ease of care. While they are "frost tender", they prefer temperatures below 68 degrees — preferably 44 to 59 degrees.

Christmas cactuses are appearing on retailers' shelves as well and these too come in many sizes. These succulent plants can be kept for another year (some are known to last for many years) and can be kept to bloom again and again with a few simple steps of retreating them to darkness and at the proper time immerging them in light to start the process of blooming again.

NATURE'S BOUNTY

Spontaneity can sometimes produce unexpected beauty in the form of wildflowers that can pop up anywhere and everywhere. They can be some of the most exhilarating because of the unusual colors, the delicacy of the blossoms, or simply their choice of location to grow.

Such was the case with a recent post by a family member via Facebook with a beauty of a picture and an inquiry as to what it was because it was growing wild and he and his wife would very much like to consider incorporating it into their wooded roadside.

The quote was "ok, since we have a couple of Master Gardeners in the family (my daughter-in-law is a Master Gardener) maybe they can help identify these flowers growing wild". I answered with my best guess and within a fraction of a second my daughter's answer popped up (nearly simultaneously) with the same answer- "Wild Phlox".

This is the time of year that they blanket the countryside with floral displays that have no rivals — they are nearly everywhere with colors ranging from white to lilac to purple to red but most, probably because of cross pollination, range in the blues.

Domesticated varieties can be purchased at retailers nearly everywhere and are similar in performance except that I think the domesticated ones are more heavily branched and produce more flowers.

You will, nearly always, be guaranteed a grand display each year be it the wild variety or the domesticated varieties.

My subject last week included the Poppy (a well-deserved subject for this time of year) but the story doesn't stop there. The Poppy has become known also as the internationally recognized symbol of remembrance. This vivid red flower has become synonymous with great loss of life in war. In more recent years it has become the symbol to help the living also — mostly those in need of help because of physical or mental hardships as a result of war.

Veteran's associations throughout the area recognize their brother's needs by asking for donations to support the cause and in turn present the 'giver' with the symbolic wired lapel red Poppy.

In the spring of 1915, when weather started to warm up the country-side, Poppies were recognized growing in the disturbed fields of Belgium and France after the cold winter. In the region around Ypres in Belgium Flanders, the spring months were unusually warm and one of the plants growing in abundance around the battle zones was the field Poppy or corn Poppy. The site of these growing on the shattered ground caught the attention of a British soldier by the name of John McCrae. He noticed how they had sprung up around the burial ground of the artillery position he was in. It is believed that he composed a poem in honor of a friend who died in battle at that time. The first lines of the famous poem have become synonymous in relation to the First World War:

> In Flanders fields the poppies blow
> Between the crosses, row on row,
> That mark our place; and in the sky
> The larks, still bravely singing, fly
> Scarce heard amid the guns below.

Each year the resting places of our loved ones and our warriors who died in battle are honored with memorial services and the placement of flags and floral displays. God bless them all!

A FLOWER WITH MANY NAMES

Typically called Surprise Lily, it is also known as Magic Lily, Resurrection Lily, and Naked Lady. They seemingly come out of nowhere in early fall, usually August in our growing zones 5 and 5 b, and are rather short lived compared to others of the Lily family. Their reference to surprise, magic, resurrection, and naked comes from the bare thick stalks that are completely void of any foliage. Their emergence to full bloom takes only four to five days and will display stalks twelve to eighteen inches tall with flower clusters of six to eight blooms of rose pink petals flushed with lavender highlights. These funnel shaped blooms are indeed a welcome "surprise" in any garden and sometimes almost forgotten until they pop up and show off in early fall. The lush gray/green foliage of these beauties arrives in the spring and dies back to an ugly and withered sand color. This makes them very adaptable to a woodland edge where their foliage becomes lost in the undergrowth or in the rear of a garden where other foliage will hide their withered remains. They will tolerate some shade but ideally grow best in a full sun-filled spot — even planted under the sod. In our climate zone, the bulbs of the Surprise Lily should be planted approximately five inches deep and six inches apart. native to China and Japan, these bulbs are hybrids and sterile because of their cross breeding, (somewhat like a mule), therefore their seeds are inconsequential, but the bulbs reproduce rapidly and can be divided every three to five years. They are a member of the Amaryllis family and the bulbs are considered poisonous.

I rather enjoy driving down country roads where these beauties are a farm favorite as I witnessed this past week. A mass planting will really catch your eye. These unique bulbs are available through internet sights, but I don't think I've ever seen them available at retailers — maybe I've just missed them. I grew them years ago having gotten the bulbs from a friend. It's one of those plants that you forget to take with you if you move because they're here and gone in a relatively short span and ultimately forgotten about until the following season.

Should you be lucky enough to attain these beauties from a friend, return the favor by passing some of the bulbs to your gardening buddies once they've started to multiply, that's what gardening buddies do, and they'll get to experience the beauty of the flower with many names — most notably "Surprise Lilly"

BEAUTY IS IN THE EYE OF THE BEHOLDER

but some flowers speak volumes as to true beauty. We all have our favorites and I have mine (Thalictrum), but then there are a few that seemingly stand out heads above some of their rivals. It might be their brilliance or maybe their colors or maybe their intricate markings, but whatever it is that strikes you, they leave a lasting impression on you.

I was attending a garden walk many years ago looking for new and unusual flowers and I wasn't disappointed when I happened onto a flower in the distance that stood out like a beacon. I had, at that time, never seen anything so brilliant (almost like a red flame), standing alone in a foundation grouping. I queried the property owner, who was helping conduct the tour, what the species name was. It was Crocosmia, which I had never heard of before and I'm thinking it was rather new in our area at the time (25 years ago). It became a "had to have" and I began my search. It was a challenge that turned out successful and was a beautiful addition in my garden. The following year I added the brilliant yellow variety as well.

The soft blue of the Butterfly Delphinium is another example of beauty at its best. Its candelabra shape and unique blue color is so awe inspiring that you have to look and look each day to drink in its beauty and hope it lasts for weeks.

Lupines are another of those unique plants that dazzle the mind with their "corn ear like" spikes that open gradually to show off their many colors of white, pink, red , and blue. A perennial, if a spot is to their liking, they will spread quite rapidly blooming in early summer. The feature plant of today's column is Foxglove (digitalis purpurea) a biennial, meaning they will produce foliage the first year and show off their blooms the following year. Sometimes, when conditions are perfect, they will bloom continually for several years. Considered poisonous to some, care should be taken to those that have susceptible conditions i.e.: allergies, skin reactions, and easy access for children. While these symptoms are rare it is good practice to heed them with caution. Foxgloves prefer a shaded to semi-shaded area with rich but well drained soil. Attaining heights two to five feet tall, they can be used in backgrounds and against fences and walls. With a few precautions they are a welcome sight in any garden because of their unique markings and their color range of white, yellow, pink, rose, red, lavender, and purple. Grow in zones 4 thru 8 for best results. They are also a great attraction for butterflies.

MAKE IT SIMPLE

Sometimes we tend to over-complicate the situation when it comes to flower beds. Three or four main groupings can be more satisfying than ten or twelve. This goes for annuals as well as perennials. With the main groupings as focal points, you can build around them with splashes of contrasting colors that will enhance that group. For example; a large bed of Rudbeckia (Black Eyed Susan) as a focal point that will scream with colors of gold and mahogany, accented with the soft blue of Russian Sage on either or both ends or, with its superior height, as a backdrop. Dot this with the blue/gray mounds of Blue Fescue Grass, evenly spaced in the foreground, used as an edging. This might be all that is necessary for a corner or any one section of your landscape.

A bed of Echinacea (Coneflower), with its soft pink petals and burnt orange to umber centers, accented with paper white Shasta Daisies and their gold centers or even the purest of whites, White Phlox, which will give you additional height if necessary. While these are just a couple examples, there are many other simple groupings that can speak volumes if handled properly. These groupings are readily available at any retailer and are perennials, so they will continue effortlessly year after year with minimal attention other than fall clean-up and occasional deadheading. A plus, also, is that they bloom continuously through-out the season.

Coreopsis is another good yellow bloomer that is very hardy and showy. I'm quite fond of Helliot-Tickseed with its "single" flat blossoms of yellow petals with strong burgundy markings toward the flower center. Another prolific Coreopsis bloomer is the double Early Sunrise variety. Moonbeam Coreopsis with its fern-like foliage and it's cousin Zagreb Coreopsis that has sturdier stems and is somewhat taller are both welcome additions to any grouping, however, expect an early flush of blooms with these two followed by intermittent blooming the rest of the season.

While the aforementioned are all perennials, the same can be said for annual beds. I've seen huge beds of Impatiens that made you crane your neck for a second look. Some were same color hues but quite often they were mixed colors of salmon, rose, violet, orange, and pink that enhanced each other and created unbelievable beauty. Another example is two or three color petunia beds that have color combinations that, quite honestly I would never have dreamed of, but someone had the ingenuity to combine them to create a masterpiece. Individualism is what makes gardening so satisfying and what makes it as popular as it has become. If you're a beginner, try your hand at different combinations of colors that are pleasing to your eye — you too might create a masterpiece.

TIRED OF THE ORDINARY

The following are really not all that unusual, but then they are not all that prevalent in most gardens either, as far as perennials go. It's fun to try different things in the garden, and sometimes it takes a little more searching to find the unusual, but that more "unusual find" can be most exhilarating when the anticipated and eventual bloom period peaks with great satisfaction.

For the "seasoned" gardener the following may be ho-hum but for those that have just begun their venture into trying new varieties, it's well worth their effort in continually trying to upgrade the new garden with some of these more difficult to find varieties.

If it's a shady area you have, try some of these perennials that bode well in semi to full shade, and I'll bet not even the "seasoned" gardeners have all of these: Leopard's Bane with its two inch yellow daisy like blooms like partial shade and will grow to two feet tall (a real stand out); Ligularia also likes partial shaded areas and produces yellow to orange blooms — space is of importance with these to allow for their wide root clumps; Toad Lily thrives in semi-shade or under a tree canopy but must be protected from early frosts with sufficient mulching; Lungwort (Pulmonaria) likes full shade and has spotted leaves that are the main attraction.

Switching to the sun-lovers: Soapwort thrives in a well-drained sunny location and produces clusters of tiny pink blooms in June, grows to six inches in height and a very attractive addition to any garden, rock garden, or border; Snow in the Summer is used like a ground-cover growing to six inches and produces profuse white blossoms with gray-green foliage; Globe Thistle deserves a spot in your garden for added interest — it bears spiny/prickly globes of gray/blue turning cerulean blue to the center — Taplow Blue is the common variety; Munstead Dwarf.

Lavender is always a must with its most desirable fragrance and subtle blue/purple florets — a native of England it is considered an herb; Balloon Flower, while more common, deserves mentioning because of its unique blossoms that form a balloon and open to a star shape while sporting a special color of blue or also creamy white alba; Oriental Daylilies, while quite common in recent years, have gained this popularity with the more recent introduction of newer and more brilliant and unusual hybrids. While these are just a few of the "not so common" perennials out there, maybe one or two would be suitable and deserve a spot in your garden- if you're like I am, it's an adventure to seek out and actually find the more unusual specimens just to admire the uniqueness and the beauty of each.

TREES AND SHRUBS

WHY DO TREES GROW WHERE THEY DO

It's fast approaching my annual trip to South Carolina for a week of golf (and hopefully warm sunshine) and it made me think about trees and how they differ from location to location.

Many states create 'state golf courses' in their forests and woodlands which typically are well maintained with the best of amenities since funds to operate these facilities are from the tax coffers. With the revenues generated from a healthy participation of eager sports enthusiasts I'm guessing they are self-supporting.

I've noticed, however, from state to state how the trees differ and have often wondered why. Through research and observation some of my questions are answered.

A state course we regularly play in South Carolina (a beauty) is predominately tall pines — I'd say at least 90%, with the rest being hardwoods. Now these trees have been there for a long period of time because of their size but I scratch my head as to why all the pines?

Well, I know for a fact that pines are prevalent in the south especially central and east coast states, because I've been to them all, but just what makes them grow there and dominate much of the land.

There's no reason other than conditions are perfect as far as soil, climate, moisture, topography, length of season, and on and on.

From the beginning of time trees grow where they do because of the aforementioned reasons but also because of past human disturbance and natural disasters over time.

How often have forests and the surrounding tundra and environment been disturbed and changed by a devastating fire or hurricane or even catastrophic ice storms. These events all play into what we have today.

We play on other courses in the south as well that are more typical of our area with many hardwood trees and sparsely dotted with pine but, for the most part, courses lean heavily to the infamous southern pine.

A few years ago I played at a state park golf course in Kentucky in the fall of the year that was probably 80% hardwoods that I kicked myself for not taking a camera. The color in the fall was a breath-taking sight in the heavily wooded rolling hills that reeked of nature at its finest.

In the northern hills of Michigan once again you are surrounded by many pines, albeit a different strain, but nonetheless in the environment they desire.

Topography plays an important role, as well, in what will grow in certain locations such as slope, aspect, and of course elevation (effective climate). In the west and higher elevations of the Rockies it's easily visible (from the tree line) where growth ends because of frigid temperatures and lack of oxygen at those levels.

Tree diseases also alter forestation and aren't limited to only certain areas. Who can't remember, other than our current generation, the wide-scale devastation caused by Dutch Elm disease? About the only good that came from this were the massive amounts of morel mushrooms that could be found.

Currently we're dealing with yet another culprit, the Emerald Ash Bore taking its toll in our surrounding area.

We pray a disease won't destroy our crown jewels — the mighty Sugar Maples of Goshen, Indiana.

"I THINK THAT I SHALL NEVER SEE A POEM LOVELY AS A TREE"

This line is from the famous American poet Joyce Kilmer's 'TREES' who wrote the poem in 1913 and first published it in 'POETRY' by Joyce Kilmer that same year. The following year it was again published in his 'TREES AND OTHER POEMS'.

The poem was probably his most notable and was dedicated to his wife's mother who was a writer in her own right and whose husband was editor of Harper's magazine.

Kilmer (born Alfred Joyce Kilmer) died at the young age of 31 while serving in the 1st World War in France, succumbing to a sniper's bullet in the 'Second Battle of the Marne' in 1918.

This poem is one of the most quoted and remembered, of his works, by literary artists. He became a much sought-after lecturer on many subjects but his first love was in poetry of which he was a prolific producer — unfortunately the literary world snubbed his works as being too simple and mundane.

Whenever I think of nature and "trees" it always brings to mind this poem. I never knew who the author was and never really researched it before but, as this business always does, it brought about discoveries that were most interesting that encouraged more and more engagement in the subject and author — one of which was the 'she' became a 'he'. Now I don't know about you, but I always considered Joyce Kilmer a 'she' until I read his biography and discovered his given name was 'Alfred' — shame on me for first impressions.

Trees are, without a doubt, one of our most valued assets in nature providing us with valued oxygen. It is said that one large mature and fully leafed tree can produce more oxygen than ten adults consume in a year, so it's not hard to understand why they are valued so much — literally, we would not survive were there not trees.

Not only are the trees that we plant so important, but also the existing forests that remain in our world are like a giant filtering mechanism for our ecosystem and the air we breathe.

Not only do trees clean the air we breathe but they also provide us with many other hidden values like filtering the soil of chemicals accidently spilled or naturally produced, their root systems control and stabilize the soil under their huge canopy as well as help control ground-water run-off — it is said they can intercept more than 1,000 gallons of water annually when fully grown, they offer a sizeable amount of noise pollution buffering when planted at strategic locations around a home or for that matter along high traffic areas or industrial parks and airports.

Trees will cool the air in a home by several degrees and reduce the need for air-conditioning while also providing a windbreak to buffer sharp winds and snows in the winter reducing heating expenses. Also, trees along with grass in any setting will bind the soil and help prevent erosion while conserving rainwater in their massive root systems.

Trees will enhance the value in your home by beautifying it and the rest of the neighborhood. Well placed valuable trees and shrubs can increase the value of a home by as much as 30%.

Well, I can't tease you with just the opening line of a poem without giving you the full-blown complete poem:

I think that I shall never see, a poem lovely as a tree.
A tree whose hungry mouth is pressed, against the sweet earth's flowing breast;
A tree that looks at God all day, and lifts her leafy arms to pray;
A tree that may in summer wear a nest of robins in her hair;
Upon whose bosom snow has lain; who intimately lives with rain.
Poems are made by fools like me, but only God can make a tree.

WHERE THERE'S SMOKE, NOT ALWAYS IS THERE FIRE

Call it what you want, Smoke Tree or Smoke Bush — it all boils down basically to how you trim and shape it. It may be purchased as a single stem tree or as a bush at most nursery and landscape growers.

Smoke Tree/Bush is one of the most handsome of the deciduous family of trees and shrubs. It also can be one of the most difficult to grow, trim, and shape.

Dead wood, nearly every year, requires pruning out to the base of the shrub (or to a pre-determined height, usually 1' to 3') where the original branching takes place. The procedure is called coppicing or stooling and is a requirement for some of your other favorites as well such as Butterfly Bush. This is a small inconvenience when one considers the over-all beauty of this landscape inclusion.

I included the specimen Royal Purple (Cotinus coggygria atropurpurea) in my island landscape addition and it never disappointed. They will produce stiff shafts of upright new growth sometimes reaching four feet in length with some of the most beautiful foliage in the landscape. If you shape the tree/shrub to encourage branching, these cut branches will make a striking focal point in a vase arrangement with other cut flowers in your home. The velvet purple of the leaves and the stout stems makes them perfect for cut flower inclusions — I liken them to eucalyptus stems only on a grander scale and, of course, a different color.

Shaping and cutting out dead wood seems to discourage many from including this beauty in the landscape but don't let this minor problem prohibit you from trying it. Just remember that this is the nature of the beast and deal with it accordingly.

If you prefer to train it as a single stem tree, more than likely you'll be trimming 'suckers' from the base of the plant on a regular basis. If kept as a shrub, each year you will trim back to your pre-determined height. You'll be amazed at the growth of 'new' shoots each season — just remember to cut them back and shape the bush to encourage more branching.

The crème de la crème is the flowering or panicles on each branch of the smoke bush that arrive during the summer as a soft magenta puff six to ten inches in length and four to six inches in diameter then eventually turning grayish white as a cloud of smoke, hence, the naming of the species.

Another of this species is the Golden Spirit Smoke Bush that produces yellow/golden/green leaves sometimes tinged with a soft red or pink. This variety will give you another option and possibly a better fit in some landscapes.

A blog I came across recently mentioned including the clematis 'Rooguchi' as a perfect fit next to Golden Spirit — its vines with indigo violet and drooping bell-shaped blooms contrasted perfectly with the green/yellow/gold of the shrub as it intertwined throughout the shrub. A perfect bonus is the remarkable fall coloring of this species that produces colors of soft yellow/orange/bronze — an unmistakable bright inclusion in any landscape planting.

Removal of dead wood and coppicing should be a spring chore only — as for shaping and 'cropping' long unsightly shoots, this chore may be done anytime — it will encourage branching to help fill in open spots in the shrub or tree.

GET IT DONE NOW

September starts the wheels turning for those fall gardening and landscape jobs. It's often asked "when is the best time to over-seed my lawn" or "when is the best time to fertilize my lawn for best results".

In fact, 'when is the best time' is probably the most often asked gardening question for any kind of gardening activity.

This one question encompasses many facets in the gardening spectrum but for now let's focus on fall.

If you would think it's too late to plant that shrub you've been wanting, you would be wrong. In fact this is the ideal time for this activity. Shrubs are normally purchased in pots, two or three gallons in size, and all are 'plant me' ready. All that is necessary is the proper fit in the landscape and the proper sized holes to receive them — twice the diameter of the pot and fifty percent deeper than the height of the pot. This planting method allows for a fresh potting soil and peat mix that will be included when planting. This allows new roots to easily establish themselves in a soft mix instead of a hard compacted soil.

Place the fresh mix in the hole to half or two-thirds its depth in a cone shaped configuration and then place the root-ball on top and wiggle it until the original plant depth is an inch or two above ground level. 'Water-in' the plant with a pre-mixed pail of root stimulator and fill the remaining hole with more of the planting mix after full absorption has taken place. The root-ball should 'settle' to its final and perfect planting depth after the final soaking.

If root 'girdling' or 'circling' was an issue when removed from the pot be sure to break the root system somewhat by twisting and pulling at the root surface but do this moderately so as not to break up the integrity of the root–ball. A utility knife may be used as another option by slicing down the sides of the root-ball to cut thru girdling roots.

Any plant, be it perennials, shrubs, trees, etc. will benefit with this technique of planting.

When considering shrubs to plant in your landscape, include one or two of these favorites. Viburnum — always a favorite but check for size at maturity because some can reach ten feet and more — I prefer the smaller varieties like Korean Spice or Carlessi; Hydrangea paniculata (vanilla strawberry is a new variety); Blue Mist Shrub — a fall bloomer; Rhododendron; Azalea; and Lilac.

Many greenhouses (especially those with year-round offerings) are heavily laden this time of year with all kinds of perennials to choose from — somewhat like a gardener's 'candy store' and most are very reasonably priced and impressive specimens.

If your plans are to plant a lawn or to simply over-seed an area that hasn't responded normally then this is the perfect time to accomplish this task. By planting now you'll be giving the new seedlings plenty of time to root before freezing takes place. Always remember new seedlings, once germinated, require a daily watering (and sometimes twice daily in dry conditions) to establish themselves. Don't take watering to extremes, however, because you're trying to establish deep rooting. If you over-water, roots tend to stay shallow and will succumb in a dry spell or a forgetful several days of non-watering. Once established, fertilize and continue the watering schedule.

For established lawns, fertilize now with a normal feeding and then again in six to eight weeks with a 'winterizer' fertilizer to establish a thick turf and an early 'green-up' in the spring.

I'VE NEVER SEEN A DOGWOOD I DIDN'T LIKE

I love dogwoods in the spring when they break color and put forth a dazzling display of soft pink or brilliant white flower petals. I love the way they are shaped with their layering of sprays and open spaces. Conformity of shape is not the norm for a dogwood — they have their own thing going on with flat layering and airy open spaces that allows light to filter into the innermost parts of this ornamental. I personally have found no other ornamental tree that is quite so beautiful as the dogwood.

Now don't get me wrong — there are plenty of other ornamental trees that are beautiful in their own right that put forth mass displays of blossoms in a range of colors that put a kaleidoscope to test, but the sheer beauty and nonconforming shape of the dogwood will fit into any landscape whether it be at the edge of a wooded setting or in a garden grouping or simply in a foundation planting. Filtered sunlight that catches these blossoms take on the appearance of glowing lights be it the pink or white variety.

Magnolia trees in the spring, when blooming, are delightful as are the Flowering Cherry, the Weeping Japanese Cherry, Flowering Crabapples of all kinds, Flowering Plum trees, and a handful of other early bloomers, but none have quite the same elegant "class" as the dogwood. What makes the dogwood an even better performer is that you get double the pleasure with their fall brilliance. Subtle colors of pink, orange, mauve, wine, yellow, as well as fire red are all part of their fall gift to a homeowner.

My first home purchased in 1957 was a small new home that had no lawn or landscaping. I hired a local friend that had just purchased an existing nursery and garden center to lay out a design for my foundation planting. Included was a dogwood of a different kind that was planned for the front corner of the house. I'd never seen a clump dogwood before but I wasn't disappointed because it turned out to be my prize plant. As beautiful as it was in the spring while blossoming, it was even more striking in the fall when it's draping six inch green leaves changed to the most brilliant red I'd ever seen in a tree (shrub). Its size increased each year to eventually reach six or seven feet in height and five feet in width. It never disappointed, spring or fall, until a number of years later when a very late spring freeze took all the tender new leaves and growth and it didn't survive — a great loss that Mother Nature dealt me.

The point of all this is to recognize the dogwood for not only its delightful spring blossoms but also for its fall performance of blazing colors as well — most of the other ornamental trees have long lost their withering leaves but the dogwood keeps on giving with a burst of fall colors that you can only imagine that fall should bring.

While not an exuberant grower, they will please anyone by the second year of growth as they establish themselves and start to develop more and more budding each succeeding year. Expect mature heights of ten to twelve feet and spreads of twelve to fifteen feet.

GOD'S PALETTE IS ALIVE AND WELL

One need only step outside or drive down a country road or visit a nursery to see the miraculous transformations of Mother Nature from summer to fall to winter. It can be a 'love-hate' relationship — love because of the brilliant brush strokes of yellows, reds, and auburns on towering trees and well placed shrubs or the fiery reds of wild roadside poison oak and clinging poison ivy on a tree or utility pole. The hates being the 'what's to follow'- the constant shoveling of snow or dealing with the sub-zero temperatures of winter. It's all about nature's way of preparing plant-life for dormancy and rest.

Well, not everyone hates the cold temps like I do (must be my age) because I would much rather be lying on a beach in bright sunshine or swinging a golf club in 90 degree weather somewhere than spinning my wheels on a snow-covered slippery road. Some people actually enjoy snow and climb mountains to slither down on skis or snowboards. I've watched younger members of my family snowboard and ski from the heights I would never even dream of climbing to in the mountains. Snow is beautiful when observing it from a nice warm inside vantage point but I'd rather not venture out into it. (Now I'm sounding like Andy Rooney).

Fall is the time that plant life full of green chlorophyll makes their yearly transformation into dormancy.

Plants feed differently than humans in that they get their food source from light, carbon dioxide, and water. They do this because, unlike humans, they are stationary and can't search for or grow their food. They create sugar to feed on and grow by this process and as a byproduct emit oxygen for humans to exist. It's a rather complicated process and too involved to print in this column but simply speaking this how the process began, to support human life. Also, since plant life can't search for water it becomes necessary for humans to supply some of the water for them to survive. The whole process is called photosynthesis and takes place in the chloroplasts, specifically using chlorophyll, the green pigment involved in photosynthesis.

Chlorophyll looks green because it absorbs red and blue light making these colors unavailable to be seen by our eyes. It's the green light that isn't absorbed that we see. In cold weather plant life and trees prepare for dormancy and since they stop feeding, the pigmentation changes thereby the yellows and reds are now visible and the greens no longer are.

Every tree and every plant we grow helps clean our air of carbon dioxide making it a win-win situation by beautifying our landscape and supporting life.

It's a beautiful world out there and we can do our part by planting trees, shrubs, and our gardens to create the oxygen we breathe and to clean the air. Plant a variety of trees so that disease and insects can't eradicate an entire area of mature trees. Seek help when a tree appears to be sick so that preventative measures can be taken to successfully restore it.

This world needs our help — let's do our part to keep it beautiful!

APPLES ARE ONE OF NATURE'S MOST BEAUTIFUL THINGS

They're not only beautiful to look at but they are one of the most nutritional fruits that nature produces, hence the old saying "an apple 'a day keeps the doctor away".

What's prettier than a bright red apple or maybe a golden yellow one with a rosy blush on the side? But then I haven't seen an apple yet that wasn't pretty as a picture, especially when you polish it.

In fact it used to be a favorite teacher's "bribe" that was always met with a big smile by any teacher worth his or her salt. That polished apple sitting on the teacher's desk meant he or she was your favorite and you deserved special privileges. Well, it doesn't always work that way but we tried.

Nutritionally speaking, they are one of the most beneficial fruits of nature because, in many ways, they assist our digestive system with fiber and natural ingredients.

A single average size apple contains 110 calories and 150 mg of potassium plus three grams of fiber which is ten percent of daily intake requirements.

While most people think that the flesh of the apple is the most delicious part, the skin of the apple is far and away the most nutritious. The apple skin contains 4 milligrams of circadian, an antioxidant compound preventing oxygen molecules from damaging individual cells. This can prevent cell changes that can lead to cancer and also lowers the risk of heart disease by twenty percent according to a study done in Finland. The study also shows that this compound has been shown to inhibit the growth of tumors and keep cancer cells from spreading.

The insoluble fiber in the apple skin is considered roughage and helps the digestive tract run smoothly and helps prevent diverticulosis, a condition that can lead to colon cancer.

Another benefit of insoluble fiber is that it helps as an appetite suppressant by giving you a "full" effect thereby acting as a weight control benefit.

Apples also contain soluble fiber, which has the opposite effect of insoluble fiber, forming a gel-like material in the digestive tract that can help lower cholesterol as well as the risk of stroke and heart disease according to the study.

Another of the soluble fibers found in apples is called pectin. Pectin reduces the amount of cholesterol produced in the liver, slows digestion, and the rise of blood sugar making it ideal for diabetes patients. Apples bolster the immune system and helps keep blood sugar levels stable.

Hundreds of new varieties of apples are researched at many of our Universities on a continuing basis with grafts and cross-breeding and most don't make the grade but some become shining stars as did a recent find. Nearly discarded and on the pile to be destroyed was one of those shining stars. It happened at the University of Minnesota when a professor pulled it from the pile to give it another "stay of execution". Understand, these grafting programs take many years to develop into a fruit producing specimen so it was a miracle indeed that this variety was saved. The "star" is non-other than the ever popular new Honey Crisp variety.

COLOR IS FOR ALL SEASONS

and cold winter months are no exception.

Landscape architects know this and will incorporate colorful twigged shrubs as well as those that will keep their foliage into the cold snowy months before eventually dropping them, thereby giving the homeowner color to enjoy throughout some of the coldest months.

If an upgrade in your landscaping is in your plans for next year, then take note of the color that you might see in existing landscapes and inquire or do some research on your own to find the species and a nursery or garden center that has or is able to obtain them. It's somewhat akin to searching in the fall for the most colorful trees to record them by name as to species and their particular breed for future use in your own plans.

Color in trees and shrubs vary from location to location, so it's not always a particular breed that will give you the brightest colors. Soil conditions, sunlight, and the surrounding environment play a big part in fall and winter color.

An example is: how often have you seen a beautiful Maple in the fall that turns brilliant red year after year before any other tree has hardly turned. It has a lot to do with the species, but more often than not it's the location and its surrounding environment.

Spirea shrubs tend to retain their colorful fall foliage late into December giving the landscape a beautiful bronze, red, and yellow coloring. Red Twig Dogwoods, after losing their soft cream and green mottled foliage, are a natural against the white winter snow showing off their bright red stems. Yellow twig Dogwoods are yet another example. Even Holly with its glossy green leaves and red berries against white snow is an eye opener. Just make sure you plant (or have in the neighborhood) a male specimen that can fertilize the female (berry producing) shrubs — in recent years hybridizing has developed a non-gender strain that has the female as well as the male pollinator and requires no outside fertilization source. Oak Leaf Hydrangeas offer purple, yellow, and orange colors in late fall — often on the same leaf. American and European Cranberry Bush not only have bright foliage but also feed wildlife, especially birds, with their purple, green, and red berries that is so necessary for them to survive.

If you have the proper location, you might try planting Bittersweet. The golden husks themselves are attractive on weaving vines, but when the husks roll back in the fall, they expose the deep orange berries that, when the vines are cut in sections, make wonderful decorations.

Winter drab is old fashioned — colorful introductions into the market are readily available at all retailer it just takes some research and imagination. Try mixing some in with your other shrubs for an injection of color.

Squirrels are burying their "stash" to prepare for their hibernation and the cold of winter, which reminds me; critters and birds alike will benefit greatly if you provide bird seed and suet so they can survive.

I used to make my own cakes by melting suet, letting it cool slightly, enough to let bird seed suspend in it, and then pouring in wax milk cartons to cool in the refrigerator. Remove from the carton and slide into a mesh bag, tying at the ends, and secure to a branch or crotch in a tree. Of course, you can simply bag chunks of suet in these same mesh bags and provide seed in a bird-feeder. Commercially prepared seed cakes are also available at retailers in the garden department. It's fun to watch all the birds and other critters and how many different varieties of birds you can attract.

WILDLIFE

EASE THE PLIGHT OF WINTER FORAGING OF OUR WILDLIFE

Our entire animal wildlife struggles through the cold and snowy winter months to survive what Mother Nature deals them.

We, as animal lovers, can help in various ways by planting the right things that invite and attract the visitors we would like to keep around. We can also erect feeders for birds and squirrels to ease their fight for survival.

While there are a multitude of trees and shrubs that produce berries in our area, some are better suited and more reveled than others by our feathered friends.

Squirrels on the other hand prefer acorns, peanuts, and corn to get them thru the harsh cold days of winter. Most will survive on their own but a little help from us will greatly enhance their survival and keep them in the landscape to enjoy their antics.

These feisty darting creatures can be loved for their acrobatic maneuvers while at the same time hated for their unwanted intrusions at the birdfeeders. Try as we might, they have a penchant for raiding the birdfeeders we erect. Many diversions have been tried (with little success) to fool or at least keep them at bay only to be outwitted again and again. I've seen birdfeeders marketed that are guaranteed to be squirrel-proof when, once erected, prove yet again that when they really want something nothing will hold them back.

Birds, chipmunks, and other small creatures may be enticed to your surroundings by creating a habitat conducive to their needs like nesting areas in trees and shrubs or 'natural' grassed area for shelter and refuge.

To make it even more critter friendly, plant fruit bearing species that are conducive to our area like flowering crabapple and cherry trees that bear small fruit. Other fruit bearing examples might include cranberry bush (any variety but some get quite large so keep maturity heights in mind), Barberry, Buckthorn, Hawthorn, Mountain Ash, Cranberry Viburnum, and Elderberry.

As for seed variety plants, any of the decorative grasses produce seed heads that birds adore, also sunflowers of all kinds, millet, and many varieties of perennials produce seeds.

I'm a bird nut, so I erected a large homemade feeder just outside my three-season room that was easily accessed and also visible from inside. I had as much fun watching the many variety of birds that visited the feeder as I did watching TV.

I was amazed at the aggressiveness of some species that I would have thought otherwise — one being the common Turtledove. I always thought Blue Jays to be the most aggressive but Doves win that battle about every time. They both like the same type of seed so the battle was on.

With selective seed purchases like black oil Sunflower seed and the 'no waste' mixture of seed, all mixed and combined before filling the feeder, little went to waste.

If you're up to the challenge try making your own suet blocks that birds crave — they're not all that difficult. Visit your local butcher and see if he can obtain a sizeable chunk of kidney suet- if possible, have him grind it for you, otherwise cut it in smaller pieces to melt in a pot on your range at a low temperature (scorching it will ruin it). If you have left-over bacon grease you may wish to mix it in also and even a little peanut butter. Pour the concoction into a container that you can easily remove it from after it is refrigerated (or frozen) and solidified- however, while it is still soft, mix in any seed of your choice and stir — I found that a quart or half-gallon milk container works well and can be cut and peeled off when solid. You may even want to roll the finished product in more seed that will adhere to the surface. Place the block in a commercial suet dispenser (cut it to fit) or ask your produce manager at the supermarket for a net 'sock' that will easily fit over the block and tie a knot at both ends. This may be wired (or tied) to a tree branch and then watch the action about to take place.

OUR WILDLIFE IS SOME OF THE BUSIEST GARDENERS ON THIS EARTH

God in his wisdom created the perfect plan for sustaining life on this earth by making gardeners out of all of us.

Humans toil to reproduce our food source each year by tilling the earth, planting the seed, and reaping the crops it produces.

Our wildlife too, unwittingly (or maybe not), till the soil, plant the seed, and reap what they sow.

Just watch the amazing activity of all the wildlife in their everyday life. They are constantly scratching or digging for food or plucking berries or fruit from a bush or tree.

Birds eat the seeds to sustain their life but in their lively activity also spread or drop seeds in other various places that will repopulate that species of plant life and on and on this activity regenerates all plant life.

Like a bird, a squirrel hunts for nuts to eat for nutrition and in the fall he too hunts voraciously for nuts to bury to sustain him through the cold winter months. Unknowingly (and maybe not) they are not all found and will sprout and grow into more trees to produce even more nuts.

Every living species has their own 'God given' plan to survive and they are very good at it, toiling endlessly day after day searching for food and unknowingly (or maybe not) by scratching, digging, and planting have perfected their own sustainability.

Every form of wildlife has a different way to not only keep their species from extinction but in the process keeps many other forms of plant life from extinction as well.

The only time this is interrupted is by a natural disaster or by human error. This is why we, as humans, have a greater responsibility to protect some of the disappearing species that we find because each has their place in God's plan.

Look at one of the efforts that have been saved from near extinction — our national symbol, the Bald Eagle. From a dwindling few they have been protected and now, with some help from us, have reproduced to the thousands. Spottings have even been found in our area which is rare indeed.

Not all creatures are seed and vegetation eaters however, some are flesh eaters — but it all remains in God's plan — the weak are eliminated and the strong survive to complete the circle and build an even stronger species. All are interconnected in one way or another to repopulate the planet and sustain life.

So, the next time you feel tired and exhausted from working in the garden or the fields, think about all the birds and the critters and the animals and the sea life with all they have to do to just stay alive — it makes our toils seem a little less significant.

All critters would appreciate a helping hand by placing seed or suet or peanuts and the like within reach to supplement their daily search for food.

On a comical note, told to me recently, was the story of several squirrels that co-operated in taking apart a fall decoration that contained several of the small decorative pumpkins and then proceeded to struggle and drag them across the yard to a nearby tree where they gorged themselves — I can't say I even knew squirrels liked pumpkin but now I know otherwise.

VEGETABLE GARDENING

GET A FRESH START ON SPRING

With the weather outside still hovering in the 20's, 30's, and 40's it's hard to visualize spring gardening, especially after just returning from South Carolina and weather in the 60's for a week of golf — it's a tough job but somebody's got to do it.

Seriously though, get a 'leg up' and dig out some of your patio pots or planters and plant a 'fresh veggie' garden and place it in a sunny location without too many drafts.

Good choices for an inside vegetable garden (while waiting for spring planting) are the hardier varieties that can withstand cold like lettuce and some of the other salad fixings.

While any type of lettuce may be used, there are varieties that add color for an indoor potted garden like the ruffled red and green leaf variety.

When weather reaches into the 40's and 50's outside, take them out and let them 'harden off' in the cool temps — just be sure to return them to the warmth inside for the evening when temps outside usually go down into the teens. These tough early veggies can handle the cold (even snow and cold rain) but not freezing weather — unless protected by a covering of snow. I've harvested lettuce a number of times when it was covered with a layer of snow but this usually happened after having a late snow in April or early May.

In another separate pot, plant some sweet basil along with some purple leaf basil to give color to a salad or even to add as a condiment to your homemade hot soup. The reason to keep this in a separate pot is that basil is extremely sensitive to cold temperatures and will frost and die very easily.

In another pot, plant some chives or green onions (if onion sets are available) to round out your salad 'fixings'.

Obviously, some of the normal ingredients of a salad will have to be purchased because of 'length of time to maturity' like tomatoes (55-70 days) or green bell peppers (70-90 days) with red, yellow, and gold bell peppers taking as long as 100 days or more.

This early experiment of growing salad fixings should probably be limited to the 'easier to grow' varieties that you can simply pluck off several leaves and toss them into a bowl and sprinkle a vinaigrette dressing or your favorite dressing at hand on them.

Don't have seeds to sow? Then trek down to your favorite garden center or big box store where they are displayed prominently in March. You'll be 'one up' on many of your gardening friends and also satisfying your gardening urge by getting your hands dirty in planting soil.

While in the gardening section browsing the seed selections, you may even see other packets of seeds that catch your eye that you may get an early start by planting now.

With early planting of longer maturing plants in an indoor environment, the most common occurrence (and fault) is lack of light and/or sunshine to keep plants from getting 'leggy'. Plants will reach for light and sun and the only way to keep them in check is to keep them in a sunny spot to keep them stocky and heavy branched. Turn them daily to keep them from leaning one way toward the light.

Good luck — and happy 'early' gardening!

COMMUNITY GARDENS ARE A BLESSING TO MANY

Community gardens are everywhere having gained popularity recently with the advent of the downturn in the economy and the need for thriftiness and prudence. Some cities are providing plots for individuals or groups to manage and reap the well-deserved harvest from all their laborious efforts of sweat and toil. Some of the participants have never had a garden and some are old hands at it, so there is a learning process that develops from this community spirit. Some say "you can't teach an old dog new tricks" but I'm a firm believer that you never stop learning when it comes to gardening. (I learn something new nearly every week). Many homeowners as well as renters have grown their gardens yearly and, by choice, have doubled these gardens in size because of economics and their willingness to share with family and friends.

If you're like I was, I always grew more than I possibly could use myself so I was constantly giving away a good deal of my crop to eager takers and, I'm sure, they were as tickled getting tomatoes, cucumbers, zucchini, beans, and onions as I was handing them out. Gardens require water and plenty of sunshine, so the ideal spot will have little, if any, shaded areas — ideally 6 to 8 hours of sunshine daily and a good source of water so that you can provide water daily if rain isn't in the forecast. One thing some gardeners fail to do is to rotate crops from year to year. As in medicine, repetition causes stagnation and eventual failure. Farmers practice crop rotation and gardeners should do likewise.

The Greencroft Community in Goshen provides small plots for their residents and they are very User friendly with easy access to a water source and plots marked off for each gardener to use as he wishes. Posts are sunken to accommodate coiled hoses and paths weave thru each plot to gain easy access for tilling and harvesting. Every garden has their specialty and run the gamut of vegetables and even some fruits. Most popular is tomatoes, zucchini, cucumbers, potatoes, and green beans.

These gardens are some of the finest because nearly all are managed by retirees that have "always" had gardens and know every trick in the book. What a blessing for these retirees to have this available at such close proximity to their residences. Large shade trees and benches are nearby to retreat for a rest and to quench their thirst. Makes for a good way to converse with your neighbors in the "Shade of the Old Apple Tree" so to speak.

Plan next year to seek out a community plot or increase your garden size to "share" with those that aren't able to have their own garden — it's a loving experience.

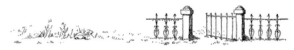

PROJECTS

JUST A LITTLE TRICK(LE) WILL DO

Do you like the sound of running or bubbling water on a warm summer day? Me too!

To me there is no sweeter sound than trickling water when kicking back and relaxing — eyes closed, feet up and a soft breeze.

You may choose to go to a public park where streams create many of these pleasing sounds or even to Lake Michigan where waves magnify the sounds. With a little ingenuity you may choose the alternative by creating your own trickling or splashing.

Some choose to go to the extreme by installing a pond with an elevated waterfall at one end or even the creation of a small stream adorned with pebbles and rocks that a pond pump can re-circulate the water from the pond and back to the top.

There is a formula to follow for the correct pump size when pumping to an elevation that any installer or pump retailer can provide you with. The length of the stream and/or the height of the waterfall or the stream will determine the size of pump necessary. Any reputable dealer will be able to provide you with pond liners, a pump or pumps, skimmer, biological filter, various spray patterns for a fountain, as well as plant baskets, clay or pond planting medium, and any plants and additives necessary to have a biologically-balanced and crystal clear pond.

An elevated and dancing stream can be achieved by purchasing a pond liner large enough to be able to cut off an end and line the stream with this excess material.

Rocks and pebbles as well as flat sheets of limestone or slate can be used to create buffers and waterfall cliffs. Long runs may require a 'weld' of two sheets of liner and dealers should be able to supply you with this kit too. I've seen some very impressive installations and all it requires is a little imagination and some 'real time' labor. Available too are long narrow strips (some even with a pebble print as a design) for your stream. To get ideas, pick up a book at the library or a book store — this is a hot topic and there are many available to choose from.

Pond installation and maintenance as well as pond plants was my chosen topic when I became a Master Gardener and community talks and demonstrations were required of you. Working as a pair, another Master Gardener and I gave numerous classes on ponds and pond plants at the library and the Ag building at the fairgrounds as well as a couple of surrounding cities.

Running or bubbling water doesn't necessarily have to be large scale. Consider even a small pot with a very small pump to create this sound — one that could easily sit on your deck or patio.

I've seen many kits available just for this purpose. A simple urn or a fancy glazed pot may also be the perfect utensil to pump from the bottom of the pot to the surface. A 3/8th inch hose (part of the kit) that runs from the pump to a surface bubbler or spray head may be regulated for strength with a simple clamp that can be tightened to the desired flow. Make sure that a tight cork is used to plug the drainage hole of an urn if this is your choice.

Impressive kits I've seen use a decorative shallow bowl where the pump is buried with pebbles. A glazed marble sphere with a hole drilled through it rests atop the pebbles. A small hose from the pump to the bottom of the sphere releases just the proper amount of water (with a flow regulator) so that a continual soft glaze of water over the shiny surface of the glazed sphere is obtained.

This is the epitome of "just a little trick(le) will do".

ARE YOU PLANNING A RAISED BED GARDEN THIS YEAR?

Well congratulations — not only for your decision to 'grow your own' but also for incorporating the raised bed design that has become so popular.

Raised bed gardens are the rave anymore because of the convenience, ease of harvesting, and the neatness they provide to a homeowner, especially city dwellers.

While any garden that is well maintained creates a visual kind of pleasure, a raised bed that is well placed in a more convenient spot like outside your back door and properly maintained will 'fit right in' to other landscaping and flower gardens.

A bed of this type doesn't necessarily have to be the 'ho-hum' garden with the standard vegetables one would ordinarily see in a garden for a food source.

Try to make your garden interesting by incorporating some unusual twists that separate it from the neighbors.

Flowers in the vegetable garden — well why not? I always ringed my garden's outer edges with alyssum (Easter Basket Mix) that gave it a more finished look. I also planted a few Marigolds to ward off insects. I filled an end with Zinnias one year (the cut-and-come-again variety) just to make the garden a little more eye appealing and Cosmos another year.

There are a number of things that you might do to set your garden off from the same 'ole, same 'ole. Purchase a teepee style trellis for a vining flower or vegetable. There are simple ones and there are elaborate ones available to choose from and it will give your garden a handsome focal point. When doing this, always keep in mind the size of your garden and don't overwhelm it with a giant behemoth.

Incorporate cement figurines for talking points like frogs, toads, turtles, angels, or fairies. Place a gazing globe in a corner spot or plant flowers in an old galvanized sprinkling can and place it in a spot that can easily be seen. In other words, make it a fun place for yourself and one that neighbors and visitors will enjoy and comment on.

One such item, in a previous article of a friend's garden, was a pair of cupped hands lying flat in the garden that contained a small amount of dirt planted with dragon's blood sedum — how neat is that? This same cement creation could contain a small amount of bird seed or simply left for water to collect in when you've watered the garden. The birds will love you for it.

When laying out a raised bed (or two or three) keep things in perspective and consider surrounding landscaping and beds — in other words don't just throw one out there. Make it a part of the whole landscape and design.

Keep beds level even if it means using more timbers on one end or cutting it into a slope in the lawn. Try to retain equal measurements between beds and use a level when laying them out and a square to keep corners even.

Raised beds planted on a slope should be cut into the slope to keep them level rather than following the slope of the landscape. It just makes sense in order to incorporate 'even' watering practices and the prevention of run-off of the soil inside the parameters of the enclosure.

ABOUT THE AUTHOR

Tom Yoder grew up in the mid-west and is a gardening enthusiast and columnist for his local newspaper. His gardening knowledge comes not only from his 16 years as a garden center manager but also his love for flowers at an early age. He also is an accomplished portrait artist winning many awards and 'Best of Show' awards. His writings depict Midwestern gardening in northern Indiana where he resides but also numerous references to plant life throughout the U.S. having visited all states but two.

DISCLAIMER: The information contained in this book is for general information purposes only. The statements contained herein have not been evaluated nor approved by the U.S. Food and Drug administration. This book is sold with the understanding the author/or publisher is not giving medical advice, nor should the information contained in this book replace medical advice, nor is it intended to diagnose, or treat any disease, illness or other medical condition.

While we endeavor to keep the information up to date and correct, we make no representations or warranties of any kind, express or implied, about the completeness, accuracy, reliability, suitability or availability, with respect to the book, or the information, products, services, for any purpose. Any reliance you place on such information is therefore strictly at your own risk.

Made in the USA
Lexington, KY
21 May 2013